Watch

THEREFORE

and

BE READY
TODAY

SECOND EDITION

DOV SCHWARZ

Watch Therefore and Be Ready Today: Second Edition

Trilogy Christian Publishers
A Wholly Owned Subsidiary of Trinity Broadcasting Network
2442 Michelle Drive, Tustin, CA 92780

Manufactured in the United States of America
10 9 8 7 6 5 4 3 2 1
Library of Congress Cataloging-in-Publication Data is available.

ISBN: 979-8-88738-261-6
E-ISBN: 979-8-88738-262-3

Table of Contents

Foreword

There are several reasons why I recommend the writings of Pastor Dov Schwarz. First, he is, first and foremost, a pastor and a shepherd of God's people. Because he has a ministry philosophy that embraces the full counsel of God's Word (Acts 20:26–27), he does not shrink away from many of the more difficult biblical issues, such as predictive prophecy, which run the risk of potentially alienating those either living in unholiness or seeking after pragmatism and relevance in our postmodern age. As a shepherd, his writings are accessible to both scholar and layman alike. He has a writing style that is engaging, enjoyable, and easy to follow.

Second, Pastor Schwarz approaches the Scripture from a distinctly Hebrew point of view. This perspective is evident not only because he is a Jewish believer in Messiah Jesus, but also because (at the time of this writing) he is currently a resident of the nation of Israel. As the Apostle Paul explained, to the Jews were given the very oracles of God (Romans 3:2). Who better to unravel the prophetic truths of God's Word than someone who also comes from this distinct cultural background?

Third, Pastor Schwarz embraces the fundamentals of Bible Prophecy. He makes no attempt to symbolize or allegorize away prophetic material that God intended to be literally construed. He also adheres to pre-millennialism (that only the Return of Christ to the earth will establish the long-anticipated millennial kingdom). He also embraces the centrality of the nation of Israel (Ezekiel 5:5; 38:12) in the outworking of God's prophetic purposes.

Beyond these essential truths, Pastor Schwarz also achieves the necessary biblical balance by demonstrating that prophecy applies directly to the daily life of the believer (2 Peter 3:11; 1 John 3:2–3). As explained by Dr. J. Dwight Pentecost, perhaps the dean of all prophecy students, God gave prophecy for the specific purpose of stimulating and motivating the daily life of the Christian. Pentecost notes:

> *"A short time ago, I took occasion to go through the New Testament to mark each reference to the coming of the Lord Jesus Christ and to observe the use made of that teaching about His coming. I was struck a new with the fact that almost without exception, when the coming of Christ is mentioned in the New Testament, it is followed by an exhortation to godliness and holy living. While the study of prophecy will give us proof of the authority of the Word of God, will reveal the purpose of God and the power of God, and will give us the peace and assurance of God, we have missed the whole purpose of the study of prophecy if it does not conform us to the Lord Jesus Christ in our daily living."* [1]

Showing how prophecy relates to daily life is a passion of Pastor Schwarz. This passion is borne out not only in the title of the present volume, *Watch Therefore and Be Ready Today*, but also in the title of his ministry, *Watch Therefore Ministries*.

This book is valuable because of its emphasis upon and exposition of the biblical covenants, the centrality of Israel in Bible Prophecy, Satan's long-standing ambition to destroy the nation of Israel in a misguided attempt to thwart God's ultimate plans, and how the world stage is currently being set up for this end time drama. Perhaps even more important is the book's emphasis upon the reader's personal involvement in these end-time events. Considering these imminent prophetic events that will soon come upon the Earth, how can the reader enter a personal relationship with their Creator, Redeemer, and the future Judge of planet Earth? How should a knowledge of these end-time events alter the believer's priorities and pattern of life in the present? In addition to communicating core prophetic subjects, these personal matters are also answered in this book. The author's passion for how these prophetic matters impact people at a personal level is self-evident in these pages. It is for reasons such as these that I recommend the writings of Pastor Schwarz in general and this volume in particular. It receives my heartiest endorsement.

— Dr. Andy Woods
Pastor-Teacher of the Sugar Land Bible Church in Houston, TX
President of Chafer Theological Seminary in Albuquerque, NM

Preface

Many years ago, while living in Houston, Texas, I founded a small ministry. This ministry still exists today but under a different name. Why? The answer to that question will unfold in the pages of this book, and I earnestly pray it will change your life and prepare you for the universe-shaking events that are upon this generation.

You see, the Holy Spirit, Who dwells in the heart, mind, and life of every truly born-again follower of Messiah Jesus, communicates to us frequently, and He certainly did so regarding the name of my ministry. He told me very clearly that He wanted me to change the ministry name to one that pertains to Bible Prophecy.

As I earnestly sought Him for that new name, I found Him to be, in my limited view, very slow about sharing exactly what it was. Approximately four years later, I was teaching a Bible study at a local church in our area on the prophetic scenarios in the New Testament book of Matthew — specifically chapter 24. Often, I would go to a special prayer room or go for a walk, praying and thinking about the passages in the Bible that I had been poring over to teach in the next few days.

I was on such a walk at the park one day when the words "watch therefore" began repeating and becoming increasingly louder in my heart and mind. Their implications became clear to me like never before. In the same way, years earlier, the Holy Spirit had told me the ministry was to receive a new name.

Without missing a step, as if no time had passed, I knew *that* was the new name of the ministry: WATCH THEREFORE!

Quite literally, my life has forever changed since that day. The words *"watch therefore and be ready"* govern and facilitate my abundant (including the good, the bad, and the ugly), exciting, and often very challenging life. This message of our Lord and Savior for this hour, if taken seriously, will fill your life with a greater understanding of your identity, purpose, calling, and grand, eternal destiny.

— Dov Schwarz
Watch Therefore Ministries

CHAPTER 1

Mountain Peaks: Covenant and Prophecy

Till I come, give attention to reading, to exhortation, to doctrine.

— 1 Timothy 4:13

Covenant

There is an old saying: "Don't make a mountain out of a molehill." But what if that saying were reversed: "Don't make a molehill out of a mountain."

As disciples of Messiah Yeshua (the Hebrew name of Jesus transliterated to English), we need to always remember that we have an ancient foe who will do anything to destroy our faith. With many millennia of experience, he has many weapons in his arsenal. One of them is attempting to deceive us into thinking that very important things in the Scriptures are unimportant. These important "things" are called doctrines, and God felt they were so important that He made it first in the list of why He gave us the Bible.

"All Scripture is given by inspiration of God, and is profitable for doctrine, for reproof, for correction, for instruction in righteousness."

— 2 Timothy 3:16

There are two doctrines that are essential but have been minimized and neglected for a long time. Covenant and Bible Prophecy are two mountain peaks that, for many in the Body of Messiah, are little more than rodent hills. This has become prevalent even amongst Christian leaders.

They claim to want to magnify and praise Jesus Christ, but most believers cannot see that the majesty of Messiah Jesus rests upon the high elevation of these majestic summits. Sadly, the most often asked question about the topic of prophecy is: "Why should I care about Bible Prophecy?" This is like someone looking straight up and asking, "Why is there snow at the top of that little molehill?"

The truth is, without a solid grasp of covenant and prophecy, the Bible is much more difficult to understand. In this often strange and modern Christian environment, many of the *"But I don't understand..."* questions would not be asked if God's people understood these two absolutely essential — dare I say the word again — doctrines.

What is *covenant* as it pertains to the Bible and the things of the kingdom of God? First, we must remember, but for a few Aramaic passages and sections, the First Testament part of the Bible was written in Hebrew. The Old Testament English word *God*, or *gods*, is translated from the Hebrew word *Elohim*. In Bible times, Elohim chose to make agreements using man's customs of the time. An agreement like this in Hebrew is *berith* (*ber-eeth*).

In the Bible, where it declares that Elohim made a covenant, in Hebrew, it is not called "making" a covenant. More accurately, it is called "cutting" a covenant. This distinction is important and affects you very personally "right now" in an eternal way. In those days, men made a covenant by cutting an animal's throat and, in many cases, walking through the animal's blood. Obviously, this is radically different from how we execute a contract today.

By walking through the blood, they were showing how serious and important the covenant was. It was taken much more seriously than our flimsy agreements today, which are sometimes disputed and taken to court. They would recite the promises of the agreement, one of which would have been: "May what happened to these animals happen to me if I break this covenant." This would make someone think twice before making and breaking covenant promises.

A covenant in the Bible is an unbreakable, immutable, unalterable agreement between two or more parties. The penalty for breaking such a covenant was death. When we think about the covenants in the Bible that Elohim made with man, we should then think of them not as just a handshake and a promise, but look on them for what they are; unbreakable, immutable, unalterable, and timeless agreements that He makes with and through His people.

A covenant would have included not only promises, terms, and conditions of agreement, but also a sign that ratified the covenant. These signs vary in the Bible depending on the covenant. Elohim cut a covenant with Noah, and what is the sign of the Noahic covenant? It is the rainbow:

> *And God said: "This is the sign of the covenant which I make between Me and you, and every living creature that is with you, for perpetual generations: I set My rainbow in the cloud, and it shall be for the sign of the covenant between Me and the earth."*
> — Genesis 9:12–13

While so many today are trying to impose various falsehoods upon, or remove so much truth from the character and ways of the God of the Bible, He has been, is, and always will be true to His covenant promises. That is so good for you and me to know that our great Father in heaven will never break His covenant promises to us.

Having said all this, let's boil down covenant to a simple and general concept. Elohim's covenants are His promises to and through His people. Covenants are God's promises.

Now, let's stand together at the base of the other mountain.

Bible Prophecy

Imagine if you had a very special, God-given talent that brought others great joy, health, and well-being. How you would feel if someone tried to take credit for your unique talent? Not only would it be very offensive to you, but (for the sake of the point I will make in a moment) it would also deprive others of receiving the benefits I mentioned. Why would it be offensive to you? Well, let's say that you lived your whole life tirelessly developing the skills and working very hard to help people with this talent.

Let's imagine that this great talent was considered by you and, more importantly, your Heavenly Father to be your life story. Then people began saying things like, "What is so important about that talent of yours?" They also began questioning the validity and changing the meaning of your life story that you'd given your heart, mind, and soul to develop. How would that make you feel? Not so good, right? I think this, in a very small way, is how our Savior feels when people question and change the meaning of Bible Prophecy.

There is a Scripture verse that demonstrates my assertion. In the book of Revelation, our Adonai Yeshua (Lord Jesus) chose an angel to give His apostle, John, a guided tour of literally earth-shaking prophetic scenarios that are coming soon to this planet and its inhabitants. This will culminate with the great marriage supper of the Lamb. As John is reeling and understandably overwhelmed, he begins to worship the angel showing him these end-time events. As we read this passage, please hear the urgency in the angel's voice regarding the significance of Bible Prophecy:

> *And I fell at his feet to worship him. But he said to me, "See that you do not do that! I am your fellow servant, and of your brethren who have the testimony of Jesus. Worship God! For the testimony of Jesus is the spirit of prophecy."*
> — Revelation 19:10

Think of this amazing truth: *the testimony of Jesus is the spirit of prophecy*. What does this mean? Have you ever heard the phrase, "the letter of the law and the spirit of the law"? It tells us that the meaning of a document or law is more than just the words that make it up; the meaning is embodied in or is in the spirit of the law. There is an overall intention for the law or document, which is the spirit of that document. For example, in legislation passed by the American Congress, this spirit is given in the introduction to the text of the law. I give you this analogy to help explain that the testimony of our Adonai Yeshua (Lord Jesus) is embodied in Bible Prophecy. The overall reason for giving His covenants in the time and way He gave them was to faithfully and miraculously keep and unfold His promises through Bible Prophecy — WOW!

There are amazing Bible Prophecy passages in the book of Isaiah. In two of them, Elohim proclaimed through His prophet in the 700s BC that a ruler would come from an empire that did not yet exist (Persia) and would be an instrument of judgment upon the Babylonian Empire. He would also fulfill other incredible prophecies regarding God's covenant people. This man, Cyrus, is mentioned by name over one hundred years before his birth.

> *Thus says the LORD to His anointed,*
> *To Cyrus, whose right hand I have held —*
> *To subdue nations before him*
> *And loose the armor of kings,*
> *To open before him the double doors, So that the gates*
> *will not be shut…*
>
> — Isaiah 45:1

Why does the God of the Bible do this with Bible Prophecy? What is so important about Bible Prophecy? Why should you care about Bible Prophecy? One very powerful reason is given in the following passage:

Remember the former things of old, For I am God,
and there is no other; I am God, and there is none like
Me,
    Declaring the end from the beginning,
    And from ancient times things that are not yet
done, Saying, "My counsel shall stand,
    And I will do all My pleasure," Calling a bird of
prey from the east,
    The man who executes My counsel, from a far
country. Indeed I have spoken it;
    I will also bring it to pass.
    I have purposed it;
    I will also do it.
— Isaiah 46:9–11

This is also explained in the verses following the mention of Cyrus:

Thus says the LORD to His anointed,
    To Cyrus, whose right hand I have held — To
subdue nations before him
    And loose the armor of kings,
    To open before him the double doors, So that the
gates will not be shut:
    "I will go before you

And make the crooked places straight;
I will break in pieces the gates of bronze And cut
the bars of iron.

I will give you the treasures of darkness And hid-
den riches of secret places, That you may know that I,
the LORD, Who call you by your name,
Am the God of Israel."

— Isaiah 45:1–3

He uses Bible Prophecy to get glory for Himself, to reveal Himself to the world as the ONLY TRUE AND LIVING GOD so that precious souls can turn to Him and be saved from destruction. Now, tell me — is that important? Bible Prophecy works hand in hand with the gospel of Messiah Yeshua to reveal His glory and majesty. Remember, the gospel of Messiah Jesus is a direct fulfillment of Bible Prophecy.

Now, back to our analogy. Abba Father gave our Savior Jesus an incredible and unique talent. Through His written word, He made promises that are thousands of years old. The people with whom He made these promises were weak and relatively few in number. Then, against all odds: the passage of time, despite the opposition of Satan and his demons — as well as those supposedly on God's side, and certainly most of the people in the world, often aggressively while unintentionally fighting against Him — He will keep those thousands-of-years-old promises, and He has precisely predicted how He will do it. This is the testimony of Jesus Christ — it is the spirit of prophecy.

Just imagine what it takes to fulfill the written prophetic scenarios. It involves moving heaven and earth to perfectly control and direct such things as peoples, empires, and world events down through the centuries. This is all being done while Satan, his demons, and most people under the sway of the wicked one (1 John 5:19) work tirelessly against Elohim. Keeping all this in mind, imagine those in the body of Messiah saying things like, "It is not important to know or care about Bible Prophecy." Some in the body of Messiah even tragically pervert and fight against His prophetic scenarios. Folks, it is downright offensive to our Savior — and in many cases, it is a direct assault upon His testimony.

The Struggle for Relevance

"We need to keep church relevant" is a slogan I have been hearing for many years as so much of the Western Church struggles in a post-Christian era. Gimmicks and clever catch-phrases tied to modern fads are the methods of the day to lure people to church. I even remember a church playing off a lingerie store chain to try to get people thinking about the gospel: "The Gospel — The *Victorious Secret*" was their Madison Avenue catchphrase. Sadly, so many have resorted to this kind of worldly gimmickry to fill the vacuum caused by the absence of preaching covenant and prophecy.

Think of these relevant issues in the world today: the global outbreak of ethnic strife and violence, the threat of nuclear war from rogue states, the global refugee crisis, radical Islamic terrorism, the Middle East crisis, rapidly changing global geopolitics, famine, pestilence, record-breaking earthquakes all over the world, the record number of persecuted and martyred Christians, societies embracing homosexual marriage, the breakdown of the traditional family, the decay and redefinition of morality, the redefining of gender, the drug overdose epidemic, abortion, and so many more.

What do all these relevant matters have in common? For one thing, they are not fun to talk about, nor are they easy to hear. The other thing is, they all point to and are the fulfillment of the end-times Bible Prophecy. Because these issues are not fun to talk about, many Christian leaders look for things that are more pleasant and appealing to discuss to bring people to church. That in itself is a fulfillment of Bible Prophecy:

> *I charge you therefore before God and the Lord Jesus Christ, who will judge the living and the dead at His appearing and His kingdom: Preach the word! Be ready in season and out of season. Convince, rebuke, exhort, with all longsuffering and teaching. For the time will come when they will not endure sound doctrine, but according to their own desires, because they have itching ears, they will heap up for themselves teachers; and they will turn their ears away from the truth, and be turned aside to fables. But you be watchful in all things, endure afflictions, do the work of an evangelist, fulfill your ministry.*
>
> — 2 Timothy 4:1–5

What are the most relevant upcoming events that will affect every person on this planet? There are so many that relevance should be the least of our problems. The biggest ones are that King Messiah Jesus is about to return to the earth and reign as the King of kings and Lord of lords, and before that, He will catch His people up in the clouds — the "Rapture"! These amazing events will change everything forever. I have a question: is that relevant? And by the way, though it involves earth-shaking events that are full of trouble, it is also very exciting to think and talk about. King Jesus is coming, and everyone on earth should be told so they can be ready.

I pray that is enough to make you want to embrace covenant and prophecy. Let's boil down Bible Prophecy to a brief, understandable concept, and then join it to our concept of *covenant*: Bible Prophecy is the way Elohim, the God of the Bible, has determined to keep His promises made to and through His people. Bible Prophecy is God's way of keeping His promises. Covenants are God's promises, and prophecy is God keeping His promises.

As we close this introductory chapter, I think there is a great way to consider the correct response to the God of Heaven regarding Bible Prophecy. Let's listen to the urgent advice given to John:

> *Worship God! For the testimony of Jesus is the spirit of prophecy.*
> — Revelation 19:10b

Understanding covenant will help us understand Bible Prophecy, which will help us worship our Father in spirit and truth (John 4:24).

CHAPTER 2

The Fathers of the Jews and Our Faith

To perform the mercy promised to our fathers and to
remember His holy covenant...

— Luke 1:72

I frequently go to Africa to lead pastor and leadership conferences. Whether I am sitting with two or standing in front of five hundred, it is an honor to share the Bible with those who teach the Good Book faithfully to so many precious souls. I almost always start by asking a question that is rarely answered correctly. I have learned this has little to do with Africa as the root of this ignorance is universal through almost two thousand years of church history.

So, are you ready? Here is the question: with whom did the Lord make the New Covenant? Think about it for a moment — what is your answer? I hear many different responses, and the two most common ones are "the Church" or "the Gentiles." But is there a place in the Bible where the question is directly answered? The answer is...YES!

Behold, the days are coming, says the LORD, when
I will make a new covenant with the house of Israel
and with the house of Judah...

— Jeremiah 31:31

When Jeremiah wrote this passage, Israel's southern and northern kingdoms were divided, yet this passage speaks of a time when a new covenant would be established under a unified Israel. So, with whom did the Lord make the New Covenant? It is clearly and unmistakably Israel. The pastors read this out loud with me and often look up with great amazement. They have been reading, living, and teaching the Bible for years but did not know with whom the Lord made the New Covenant. Before explaining how this happened, let's back up and start with the fathers of the Jewish people and of all those who call Jesus Christ their Savior.

Fathers Abraham, Isaac, and Jacob

The Name "LORD" in capital letters refers to the Hebrew letters from which we get the English terms Yahweh or Jehovah. In English, the Hebrew letters are transliterated as "YHVH." This is all very Israeli, right? Genesis chapters 12 and 15 record that the LORD God (Yahweh Elohim) called a man named Abram and cut a covenant with him.

This covenant includes very specific terms by which both parties can activate and maintain the covenant, its promises, the walk through the blood, and the covenant sign. Whether Jew or Gentile, there are promises for you in this covenant. If you are a non-Jewish follower of Messiah Jesus reading this book right now, you are a direct fulfillment of the seventh promise — excuse me a moment — HALLELUJAH!

> *Now the LORD had said to Abram: "Get out of your country,*
>> *From your family*
>> *And from your father's house, To a land that I* *will show you. I will make you a great nation; I will bless you*
>> *And make your name great; And you shall be a* *blessing.*
>> *I will bless those who bless you*
>> *And I will curse him who curses you;*
>> *And in you all the families of the earth shall be* *blessed."*
>
> — Genesis 12:1–3

Let's identify seven promises that pertain to Abram as he leaves all he knows to follow Elohim to a land that He will show him:

1. Elohim will make Abram a great nation.
2. Elohim will bless Abram.
3. Elohim will make the name of Abram great.
4. Elohim will make Abram a blessing.
5. Elohim will bless those who bless Abram.
6. Elohim will curse those who curse Abram. There are two different words used for the word "curse." The one pertaining to those who curse Abram means "to esteem lightly" and is used

this way in 1 Samuel 2:30; 18:23; Isaiah 9:1 in the New King James Version.

7. Elohim will bless people all over the world through Abram.

In Genesis 15, we see that Abram, who is in his 70s and has a barren wife, is worried about how this will all take place since he has no children to pass these covenant promises through.

After these things the word of the LORD came to Abram in a vision, saying, "Do not be afraid, Abram. I am your shield, your exceedingly great reward."

But Abram said, Lord God, what will You give me, seeing I go childless, and the heir of my house is Eliezer of Damascus?" Then Abram said, "Look, You have given me no offspring; indeed one born in my house is my heir!"

And behold, the word of the LORD came to him, saying, "This one shall not be your heir, but one who will come from your own body shall be your heir." Then He brought him outside and said, "Look now toward heaven, and count the stars if you are able to number them." And He said to him, "So shall your descendants be."

And he believed in the LORD, and He accounted it to him for righteousness.

— Genesis 15:1–6

The key for entering covenant with the LORD God is in the sixth verse, where it shows how Abram became righteous

— not guilty but forgiven and granted eternal life — he believes Elohim; that's it. Abram decided to walk by faith and not by sight. In all but one of the covenants, believing is what one must do to experience the covenant benefits from the Creator of the universe — once again — Hallelujah! Truly, this affects you right where you are right now. Are you believing and trusting in the LORD God today?

Abram continues to discuss these things with Elohim:

And he said, "Lord God, how shall I know that I will inherit it?"

So He said to him, "Bring Me a three-year-old heifer, a three-year-old female goat, a three-year-old ram, a turtledove, and a young pigeon." Then he brought all these to Him and cut them in two, down the middle, and placed each piece opposite the other; but he did not cut the birds in two. And when the vultures came down on the carcasses, Abram drove them away.

Now when the sun was going down, a deep sleep fell upon Abram; and behold, horror and great darkness fell upon him. Then He said to Abram: "Know certainly that your descendants will be strangers in a land that is not theirs, and will serve them, and they will afflict them four hundred years. And also the nation whom they serve I will judge; afterward they shall come out with great possessions. Now as for you, you shall go to your fathers in peace; you shall be buried at a good old age. But in the fourth generation they shall return here, for the iniquity of the Amorites is not yet complete."

And it came to pass, when the sun went down and it was dark, that behold, there appeared a smoking oven and a burning torch that passed between those pieces. On the same day the LORD made a covenant with Abram, saying:

"To your descendants I have given this land, from the river of Egypt to the great river, the River Euphrates — the Kenites, the Kenezzites, the Kadmonites, the Hittites, the Perizzites, the Rephaim, the Amorites, the Canaanites, the Girgashites, and the Jebusites."

— Genesis 15:8–21

In His great kindness and love, the LORD comes down from His high and holy place to enter into man's customary way of making official agreements. He takes on the tangible form of a smoking oven and torch. If you study the Scriptures, you will find many explanations for these elements, but for our purposes, we will just acknowledge that Elohim came down to cut a covenant with Abram. We see the cut animals — and it would have been a bloody mess, frankly speaking. We see the two parties, but only one of them walks through the blood. Why is this? The answer is very interesting.

Conditional vs. Unconditional Covenant?

People in theological discussions debate this matter. Some say the Abrahamic Covenant and the other covenants in the Bible, except for one, are unconditional. Unconditional means that only one of the parties is responsible for keeping the covenant terms. Some say that since Abram does not walk through the blood, he is not obligated to keep the terms of the agreement. This means only the LORD is responsible, which expresses grace, which is unconditional. Others believe that since Abram left his home and family to go out in faith, this was his part of the covenant. And since it is true that one must repent or turn from his old direction of sin and disobedience to the LORD — this is a condition to be kept.

This much we know: Abram did not walk through the blood, so only one party is obligated to keep the terms of this agreement, right? Additionally, the LORD said, "I will," and did not say, "I will if you will," while stating the terms. Yes, Abram had to leave his old life to position himself to enter into the covenant, and if you want to call that a condition — fine with me. But let's also agree that nobody can perfectly keep a covenant with God. Had this agreement been conditional upon Abram's keeping it perfectly, he would have been a dead man. Also, let's remember that Abram's righteousness was accounted to him for believing in the LORD — and the same is true for you today if you believe.

Important Note: The Great Nation Has Boundaries

The first of the seven promises to Abraham was a great nation. A great nation must have national people and clear boundaries. In Genesis 15, the LORD tells Abraham and the entire world the boundaries of this great nation. Remember the word "relevance"? This is so relevant that it is shaking the earth today, and it is just the beginning. Stick around, and by the time you are finished reading this book, I challenge you to find anything more relevant to earth's inhabitants.

Abram to Abraham and the Child of Promise

In Genesis 16, Abram and Sarai get tired of waiting for this child who will inherit all these promises. Abram is also probably getting a bit desperate, being ninety-nine years old; and his barren wife is no spring chicken either. So, the two of them walk out this cooked-up plan to help Elohim keep His promises. Abram will have relations with Sarai's maidservant, and Sarai will be a very hands-on midwife, which would constitute, in their mind, fulfilling the promise from the LORD.

The problem is — this was not God's plan to fulfill the promises. I heard a pastor once say, "God does not only feel that His way is the best way. He feels that His way is the ONLY way!" So, Abram and his wife make an "Ishmael." Ishmael is one of the primary fathers of the Middle East. To find out why we have all the problems in the Middle East that are the focus of nearly every news cycle, listen to the word of the LORD as He speaks of Ishmael:

> *He shall be a wild man; His hand shall be against*
> *every man, And every man's hand against him. And*
> *he shall dwell in the presence of all his brethren.*
> — Genesis 16:12

I say, "they made an Ishmael" because, for all of us, this represents trying to do the right thing the wrong way, which can bring disastrous results and unintended consequences. We can learn from Abram's mistake and know that the LORD can help us go forward when we make an Ishmael. By the way, the LORD loved and blessed Ishmael, and He loves and wants to make a way for his descendants today.

This little detour did not prevent the LORD from keeping His covenant promises — the child of promise was on the way. He would come from the father of many nations — Father Abraham. Let's see the way forward from the LORD:

As for Me, behold, My covenant is with you, and you shall be a father of many nations. No longer shall your name be called Abram, but your name shall be Abraham; for I have made you a father of many nations.
— Genesis 17:4–5

Abram means "father of many," while Abraham means "father of multitudes."

And God said to Abraham: "As for you, you shall keep My covenant, you and your descendants after you throughout their generations. This is My covenant which you shall keep, between Me and you and your descendants after you: Every male child among you shall be circumcised; and you shall be circumcised in the flesh of your foreskins, and it shall be a sign of the covenant between Me and you."
— Genesis 17:9–11

Circumcision is the sign of the covenant.

Then God said to Abraham, "As for Sarai your wife, you shall not call her name Sarai, but Sarah shall be her name. And I will bless her and also give you a son

by her; then I will bless her, and she shall be a mother
of nations; kings of peoples shall be from her."

Then Abraham fell on his face and laughed, and
said in his heart, "Shall a child be born to a man who
is one hundred years old? And shall Sarah, who is
ninety years old, bear a child?" And Abraham said to
God, "Oh, that Ishmael might live before You!"

— Genesis 17:15–18

Is Ishmael the child of promise?

Then God said: "No, Sarah your wife shall bear you a
son, and you shall call his name Isaac; I will establish
My covenant with him for an everlasting covenant,
and with his descendants after him."

— Genesis 17:19

Think of this: God is going to use a one-hundred-year-old man and his barren, elderly wife to populate the planet with children of the Most High God — Hallelujah! Notice that our Creator clearly tells Abraham and us that the covenant will come through Isaac, not Ishmael. We will see that this is very important for everyone on the planet today — very relevant.

The Child of Bible Prophecy

And the LORD visited Sarah as He had said, and the
LORD did for Sarah as He had spoken. For Sarah
conceived and bore Abraham a son in his old age, at
the set time of which God had spoken to him. And

Abraham called the name of his son who was born to him — whom Sarah bore to him — Isaac. Then Abraham circumcised his son Isaac when he was eight days old, as God had commanded him. Now Abraham was one hundred years old when his son Isaac was born to him. And Sarah said, "God has made me laugh, and all who hear will laugh with me." She also said, "Who would have said to Abraham that Sarah would nurse children? For I have borne him a son in his old age."

— Genesis 21:1–7

This is Bible Prophecy! This is the LORD demonstrating to the inhabitants of the world Who He is. He is able to do — and will do — the impossible, according to His word. He made promises to Abraham and is keeping them according to His prophetic word — this is Bible Prophecy — what a great and mighty Elohim we serve!

Isaac, the promised child, brings forth and fulfills the Abraham Covenant as he fathers the next child, who will carry forth the covenant promises. In New Covenant times and passages, we learn that Isaac is an Old Testament type or picture of the greatest Promised Child. Bible Prophecy fulfills the promises as Isaac's wife Rebecca struggles with two nations in her womb:

But the children struggled together within her; and she said, "If all is well, why am I like this?" So she went to inquire of the LORD.

And the LORD said to her:

"Two nations are in your womb, Two peoples shall be separated from your body; One people shall be stronger than the other, And the older shall serve the younger."

So when her days were fulfilled for her to give birth, indeed there were twins in her womb.

— Genesis 25:22–24

Remember what the LORD promised Abraham? These same promises were transmitted through Isaac and his descendants. In Rebecca's womb, there was a struggle between two what? They are not two babies, but two nations of peoples. We will see later through Bible Prophecy that one is the covenant nation and the other becomes a nation that tries to destroy the covenant promises. The covenant child was named Jacob, and the destroyer's name was Esau. Look at what the LORD says about them as Paul the apostle in the New Covenant Scriptures quotes the Old Testament prophet Malachi:

As it is written, "Jacob I have loved, but Esau I have hated."

— Romans 9:13

But wait a moment, God is love, right? How could the LORD not love Esau? The verse is not only a reference to a person but also a nation of key people who carry out Satan's work to destroy the covenant promises of God. Not only are Esau's descendants and the demonic spirits they harbor a threat to the promises — they will fulfill Bible Prophecy.

Dear friends, this is so very relevant for today. The same spirit that possessed and controlled Esau is controlling many people in this generation. This should be a warning to the inhabitants of the earth today, as Bible Prophecy leaps off the pages and the covenant promises are being fulfilled in our generation. Keep reading — you will see!

Esau did not care about the covenant the LORD made with his father Isaac. He was a carnal man who began with indifference to the LORD and His covenant. His disregard for Elohim was expressed by trading his firstborn inheritance of the covenant promises for a bowl of stew. Talk about trading something for nothing! To whom did he trade his destiny for a bowl of stew? He traded it to Jacob — the one who represented the great covenant nation in Rebecca's womb.

> *Now Jacob cooked a stew; and Esau came in from the field, and he was weary. And Esau said to Jacob, "Please feed me with that same red stew, for I am weary." Therefore his name was called Edom. But Jacob said, "Sell me your birthright as of this day." And Esau said, "Look, I am about to die; so what is this birthright to me?" Then Jacob said, "Swear to me as of this day." So he swore to him, and sold his birthright to Jacob. And Jacob gave Esau bread and stew of lentils; then he ate and drank, arose, and went his way. Thus Esau despised his birthright.*
>
> — Genesis 25:29–34

Notice that from this time forward, Esau is associated with the name of the red stew (Edom means "red") for which he traded a relationship with Elohim. He never recovered from this exchange of the temporary instead of the eternal Elohim and His covenant blessings. The writer of the New Covenant book of Hebrews warns us of the consequences of Esau's choice:

> *For you know that afterward, when he wanted to inherit the blessing, he was rejected, for he found no place for repentance, though he sought it diligently with tears.*
>
> — Hebrews 12:17

This, of course, speaks of the time when Rebecca, knowing her sons and the covenants the LORD had made with Isaac, talks Jacob into deceiving Isaac. Isaac's poor eyesight and illness provide an opportunity to trick him into passing the covenant promises to Jacob. Isaac sends Esau out to hunt food, telling him that upon his return, he will pray the covenant blessing over him. Hearing this, Rebecca tells Jacob to prepare two goats and take them to Isaac while pretending to be Esau:

> *And Jacob said to Rebekah his mother, "Look, Esau my brother is a hairy man, and I am a smooth-skinned man. Perhaps my father will feel me, and I shall seem to be a deceiver to him; and I shall bring a curse on myself and not a blessing."*
> *But his mother said to him "Let your curse be on me, my son; only obey my voice, and go, get them for me." And he went and got them and brought them to his mother, and his mother made savory food, such as*

his father loved. Then Rebekah took the choice clothes
of her elder son Esau, which were with her in the
house, and put them on Jacob her younger son. And
she put the skins of the kids of the goats on his hands
and on the smooth part of his neck. Then she gave the
savory food and the bread, which she had prepared,
into the hand of her son Jacob.

    So he went to his father and said, "My father."
And he said, "Here I am. Who are you, my son?"

    Jacob said to his father, "I am Esau your firstborn;
I have done just as you told me; please arise, sit and
eat of my game, that your soul may bless me."

    — Genesis 27:11–19

This is followed by the blessing and passing of the covenant to Jacob.

    Then his father Isaac said to him, "Come near now
and kiss me, my son."

    And he came near and kissed him; and he smelled
the smell of his clothing, and blessed him and said:

    "Surely, the smell of my son Is like the smell of a
field Which the LORD has blessed. Therefore may God
give you Of the dew of heaven, Of the fatness of the
earth, And plenty of grain and wine. Let peoples serve
you, And nations bow down to you. Be master over
your brethren, And let your mother's sons bow down
to you. Cursed be everyone who curses you, And blessed
be those who bless you!"

    — Genesis 27:26–29

Later in this chapter, when Esau learns of this deception, Isaac tells Esau that his brother deceived him. Isaac and Esau agree that Jacob deceived them, but they also acknowledge that the blessing cannot be reversed. What is the LORD doing here, and how can deception like this be blessed?

I am going to give four answers to this question and then move on:

1. Esau despised his birthright.
2. We must not forget about Rebecca's significant influence.
3. The LORD is working His plans through a very sinful earth full of very corrupt people — like you and me!
4. Just like with us, the LORD brings trials into Jacob's life to humble and change him.

It is through a very different struggle that we first hear the name of the covenant nation. Jacob is on his way to meet Esau for the first time after the events mentioned above. The last Jacob heard was that Esau wanted to kill him. Jacob now has a large family and is moving toward the covenant land when he encounters a theophany, or a human visitation from the LORD, and he wrestles with Him for a blessing.

> *Then Jacob was left alone; and a Man wrestled with him until the breaking of day.*
> *Now when He saw that He did not prevail against him, He touched the socket of his hip; and the socket of Jacob's hip was out of joint as He wrest-*

*led with him. And He said, "Let Me go, for the day
breaks."*

*But he said, "I will not let You go unless You bless
me!"*

So He said to him, "What is your name?"

He said, "Jacob."

*And He said, "Your name shall no longer be called
Jacob, but Israel; for you have struggled with God and
with men, and have prevailed."*

*Then Jacob asked, saying, "Tell me Your name, I
pray."*

*And He said, "Why is it that you ask about My
name?" And He blessed him there.*

*So Jacob called the name of the place Peniel: "For I
have seen God face to face, and my life is preserved."*

— Genesis 32:24–30

From this time forward, Jacob walks with a limp. He humbles himself before Esau, and as you read through his very difficult life, you will notice a marked difference in his character. For the rest of his life, we see brokenness in His body, having wrestled with the LORD. This is what must happen in our hearts to truly walk with Messiah Yeshua. Many years ago, I heard a saying referencing this kind of godly humility: "Never trust a man who does not walk with a limp."

The covenant is passed from Abraham to Isaac and then to Jacob/Israel. The Bible calls them "fathers," as they are the fathers of our faith. There are New Covenant (also called New Testament) passages that tell us Abraham is the spiritual father of all who have faith in Messiah Jesus:

Now I say that Jesus Christ has become a servant to the circumcision for the truth of God, to confirm the promises made to the fathers...

— Romans 15:8

Therefore know that only those who are of faith are sons of Abraham. And the Scripture, foreseeing that God would justify the Gentiles by faith, preached the gospel to Abraham beforehand, saying, 'In you all the nations shall be blessed.' So then those who are of faith are blessed with believing Abraham.

— Galatians 3:7–9

Some of the Jewish people came against the gospel, which Paul tells us catapulted the good news to the nations of the world. He explains how this enmity toward the gospel was all in God's plan and for the sake of the Gentiles, as they benefited by having the opportunity to hear the good news. Yet the Lord loves the Jewish people, and look at the root of that love — it is for the sake of Abraham, Isaac, and Jacob/Israel, the fathers.

Concerning the gospel they are enemies for your sake, but concerning the election they are beloved for the sake of the fathers.

— Romans 11:28

CHAPTER 3

Covenant: Moses, David, New

*For whatever things were written before were writ-
ten for our learning, that we through the patience and
comfort of the Scriptures might have hope.*

— Romans 15:4

The Moses (Mosaic) "If you will" Covenant

The next covenant the LORD made, or cut, with the children of Israel was through His great deliverer, Moses.
This is where we get the terms "the law" and "priests" or "priesthood." The priesthood comes through the Israeli tribe of Levi,
and the high priest is through a descendant named Aaron. In
the book of Exodus, we see the shedding of blood not only to
cut the covenant but also as a sign, beginning with the blood
of the Passover Lamb.

How did all this come to pass? It is through the prophetic
word of the LORD: Bible Prophecy. In Genesis 15, the prophetic word came to Father Abraham regarding the children of
Israel being sent out of the Promised Land. Due to the Joseph
scenario later in Genesis, just as foretold to Abraham, there
they were — in Egypt. After Joseph's passing, the children of

Israel served the Egyptians as horribly afflicted slaves for four hundred years, just like Bible Prophecy said.

The LORD told Pharaoh through Moses, "Let My people go," yet the Egyptian leader was stubbornly defiant. Then came nine ferocious plagues — each one a judgment on the false gods of Egypt. The final plague was a death sentence upon the firstborn of man and animal across Egypt. We often forget that Israel is the firstborn son of the LORD. According to the Abraham Covenant, the LORD cursed Egypt.

> *Then you shall say to Pharaoh, "Thus says the LORD: 'Israel is My son, My firstborn. So I say to you, let My son go that he may serve Me. But if you refuse to let him go, indeed I will kill your son, your firstborn.'"*
> — Exodus 4:22–23

The LORD is about to judge the Egyptians with a tenth and final plague. This will force their leader Pharaoh to let Elohim's people go. The wrath of God will pass over every home that has the blood of an unblemished lamb on the doorposts.

> *Now the blood shall be a sign for you on the houses where you are. And when I see the blood, I will pass over you; and the plague shall not be on you to destroy you when I strike the land of Egypt.*
> — Exodus 12:13

Later in the book of Exodus, the children of Israel collectively agree to the condition often referred to as the Moses

Covenant. Notice that they fully embrace a willingness to keep the terms of the covenant.

In the third month after the children of Israel had gone out of the land of Egypt, on the same day, they came to the Wilderness of Sinai. For they had departed from Rephidim, had come to the Wilderness of Sinai, and camped in the wilderness. So Israel camped there before the mountain.

And Moses went up to God, and the LORD called to him from the mountain, saying, "Thus you shall say to the house of Jacob, and tell the children of Israel: 'You have seen what I did to the Egyptians, and how I bore you on eagles' wings and brought you to Myself. Now therefore, if you will indeed obey My voice and keep My covenant, then you shall be a special treasure to Me above all people; for all the earth is Mine. And you shall be to Me a kingdom of priests and a holy nation.' These are the words which you shall speak to the children of Israel."

So Moses came and called for the elders of the people, and laid before them all these words which the LORD commanded him. Then all the people answered together and said, "All that the LORD has spoken we will do." So Moses brought back the word of these people to the LORD.

— Exodus 19:1–8

Israel's great blessings were associated with keeping the terms of the Moses Covenant. Yet there were also sure and certain curses and a need for a New Covenant that would fol-low Israel's turning away from their sacred requirements. There are many passages that warned Israel's descendants that their generation, and many to come, would be removed from the covenant land if they forsook this covenant. Here is a brief snapshot of these blessings and curses:

> *Now it shall come to pass, if you diligently obey the voice of the LORD your God, to observe carefully all His commandments which I command you today, that the LORD your God will set you high above all nations of the earth. And all these blessings shall come upon you and overtake you, because you obey the voice of the LORD your God:*
>
> *Blessed shall you be in the city, and blessed shall you be in the country.*
>
> *Blessed shall be the fruit of your body, the produce of your ground and the increase of your herds, the increase of your cattle and the offspring of your flocks.*
>
> *Blessed shall be your basket and your kneading bowl.*
>
> *Blessed shall you be when you come in, and blessed shall you be when you go out.*
>
> *The LORD will cause your enemies who rise against you to be defeated before your face; they shall come out against you one way and flee before you seven ways.*
>
> *The LORD will command the blessing on you in your storehouses and in all to which you set your hand,*

and He will bless you in the land which the LORD your God is giving you.

— Deuteronomy 28:1–8

But it shall come to pass, if you do not obey the voice of the LORD your God, to observe carefully all His commandments and His statutes which I command you today, that all these curses will come upon you and overtake you:

Cursed shall you be in the city, and cursed shall you be in the country.

Cursed shall be your basket and your kneading bowl.

Cursed shall be the fruit of your body and the produce of your land, the increase of your cattle and the offspring of your flocks.

Cursed shall you be when you come in, and cursed shall you be when you go out.

The LORD will send on you cursing, confusion, and rebuke in all that you set your hand to do, until you are destroyed and until you perish quickly, because of the wickedness of your doings in which you have forsaken Me. The LORD will make the plague cling to you until He has consumed you from the land which you are going to possess.

— Deuteronomy 28:15–21

Then the LORD will scatter you among all peoples, from one end of the earth to the other, and there you shall serve other gods, which neither you nor your

fathers have known — wood and stone. And among
those nations you shall find no rest, nor shall the sole
of your foot have a resting place; but there the LORD
will give you a trembling heart, failing eyes, and an-
guish of soul. Your life shall hang in doubt before you;
you shall fear day and night, and have no assurance
of life. In the morning you shall say, "Oh, that it were
evening!" And at evening you shall say, "Oh, that it
were morning!" because of the fear which terrifies your
heart, and because of the sight which your eyes see.

— Deuteronomy 28:64–67

We know from history that this is exactly what the LORD did when Israel rebelled against Him and broke the Moses Covenant. But even in this, the LORD has a plan, and He has not forgotten His promises to and through Abraham, Isaac, and Israel. In the Moses Scriptures, we also see the promise to re-gather the Jewish people. Circumcision in the flesh, which is the sign of the Abraham Covenant and a command of the Moses Covenant, will later be turned inward for the Jewish people, becoming a circumcised heart that truly loves the LORD God. The God of Israel will gather the Jewish people from the nations and change the hearts of a remnant that He has preserved (Romans 15:25–27). The effects of these things are in the news every day, all over the world — these are today's headlines!

If any of you are driven out to the farthest parts under
heaven, from there the LORD your God will gath-
er you, and from there He will bring you. Then the

LORD your God will bring you to the land which
your fathers possessed, and you shall possess it. He will
prosper you and multiply you more than your fathers.
And the LORD your God will circumcise your heart
and the heart of your descendants, to love the LORD
your God with all your heart and with all your soul,
that you may live.

— Deuteronomy 30:4–6

The David (Davidic) Covenant: A Man After God's Own Heart

In the first century, in Jericho, a very controversial Man walks down a busy street which is full of more people than usual. It is a chaotic scene, and this Man is the reason for the upheaval. Some say He is a prophet, others accuse Him of being a deceiver, while others say He is the long-awaited Messiah of Israel.

There is another fellow on that road who is the last person anyone would ask regarding the identity of this Man of interest. The reason few will consider this unlikely fellow as *in the know* is because he is a blind beggar. His name is Bartimaeus. The eyes in his head may be without sight, but he has eyes that bring pleasure to the LORD our God, the eyes of faith. Well, our disregarded friend has plenty of that kind of sight.

And what is this sound from his soul, piercing the chaos and giving evidence that his spiritual eyes and ears can see and hear?

Now they came to Jericho. As He went out of Jericho with His disciples and a great multitude, blind Bartimaeus, the son of Timaeus, sat by the road begging. And when he heard that it was Jesus of Nazareth, he began to cry out and say, "Jesus, Son of David, have mercy on me!"

— Mark 10:46–47

Why did our dear brother Bartimaeus cry out for mercy to Jesus of Nazareth? Why did he call Jesus the Son of David? To know the answer, we need to understand the David Covenant.

King David was in his beautiful house of cedar and felt in his heart that he should build a house for the LORD for the ark of the covenant to dwell. However, it was the LORD's plan to have his son, Solomon, build such a house, which turned out to be a grand temple. When Elohim sent His prophet Nathan to share these things with David, He gave Israel's king an exciting prophetic word. It is important to notice that we will see Solomon used as an Old Testament type or shadow of the eternal King.

"When your days are fulfilled and you rest with your fathers, I will set up your seed after you, who will come from your body, and I will establish his kingdom. He shall build a house for My name, and I will establish the throne of his kingdom forever. I will be his Father, and he shall be My son. If he commits iniquity, I will chasten him with the rod of men and with the blows of the sons of men. But My mercy shall not depart from him, as I took it from Saul, whom I

removed from before you. And your house and your
kingdom shall be established forever before you. Your
throne shall be established forever." According to all
these words and according to all this vision, so Na-
than spoke to David.

— 2 Samuel 7:12–17

We can glean from this passage that the eternal Son will come from the physical line of David and sit on his throne forever. The kingdom of David will be the Eternal Kingdom of the LORD. We also see the physical beating Messiah will take for the iniquities of Solomon and all of us. Obviously, nobody ever beat King Solomon for his iniquities — that would have been a suicide mission — but one day they gave blows to the only begotten Son of God because Abba Father sent Him for that purpose. So there will be a Son of David who will forever reign and rule as King over Israel. He will build a new and glorious house for the LORD. His will be an eternal kingdom that will never pass away. This is the Son of David!

Our friend Bartimaeus, who is not so blind after all, is saying that he believes this is the Messiah, the Savior of Israel; the Eternal King who will rule and reign from David's throne forever. Messiah Jesus restores Bartimaeus' physical eyesight as a result of his great faith — Hallelujah! By the way, if you are looking for some interesting study of the David Covenant, the Old Testament prophet Ezekiel, chapters 40–48, explains this Temple of the LORD in great detail.

As the Bible unfolds, we begin to see Yahovah (LORD), also called *Adonai*, which is translated into English as "Lord." From what we see in the Bible, this most often refers to King

Messiah Jesus in heaven before His first-century ministry. Finally, regarding the David Covenant — David was known and spoken of by the Lord as a man after God's own heart. Samuel says to King Saul, who will soon be deposed by the LORD:

> *And Samuel said to Saul, "You have done foolishly. You have not kept the commandment of the LORD your God, which He commanded you. For now the LORD would have established your kingdom over Israel forever. But now your kingdom shall not continue. The LORD has sought for Himself a man after His own heart, and the LORD has commanded him to be commander over His people, because you have not kept what the LORD commanded you."*
> — 1 Samuel 13:13–14

It is often correctly taught that though David had a couple of major sinful failures, his overall life was one of heartfelt love for the Lord. When he sinned, David always repented with great sorrow, confession of sin, and a change of direction. Yet there is another reason David is a man after Elohim's own heart: he is a type or Biblical Old Testament shadow of Messiah Jesus. Remember, our Adonai Jesus is the Son of David. What could be more after our Savior's own heart than Himself sitting on David's throne in Jerusalem? What could touch the heart of our Father in heaven more than His only begotten Son, in whom He is well pleased, sitting on the throne of David?

This raises a question that leads to a David Covenant answer. Where is Messiah Jesus now? Yes, He is in heaven — but where in heaven? He is sitting on our Father's throne:

To him who overcomes I will grant to sit with Me on My throne, as I also overcame and sat down with My Father on His throne.

— Revelation 3:21

This passage speaks of a future day when Messiah Jesus will be sitting on His throne. Today, however, He sits with His Father on His throne. Why is our Messiah Jesus waiting to sit on His own throne? It is because He is waiting to sit on the throne of David in Jerusalem to fulfill the David Covenant — Hallelujah!

The Crown Jewel — The New Covenant

There are so many aspirations and accomplishments that man tirelessly seeks. World-class competitions, records of achievement, prizes and trophies with widespread prestige are pursued and marketed around the globe. But there is nothing comparable to what was accomplished by Elohim's establishing of the New Covenant. God the Father, Son, and Holy Spirit employed heavenly hosts — even Satan himself and his cohorts unwittingly helped the Creator of the universe — to usher in the greatest accomplishment in human history.

Think of it — before the foundation of the world, all the New Covenant details were planned to pinpoint accuracy, to the last and most minute detail. Consider all the moving parts: people, places, things, events, etc. Not only every covenant promise but all the previous covenant pictures and shadows had to be fulfilled perfectly by Messiah Jesus in the New Covenant.

Consider the Passover: in Egypt, the children of Israel were instructed regarding what would be the beginning of their new lives and the beginning of each new year. As previously mentioned, they were commanded to keep a lamb without blemish for four days and then kill it. They would then take the blood and strike the doorposts with it. This would ensure that the wrath of the LORD would pass over their houses:

> *Now the LORD spoke to Moses and Aaron in the land of Egypt, saying, "This month shall be your beginning of months; it shall be the first month of the year to you. Speak to all the congregation of Israel, saying: 'On the tenth of this month every man shall take for himself a lamb, according to the house of his father, a lamb for a household. And if the household is too small for the lamb, let him and his neighbor next to his house take it according to the number of the persons; according to each man's need you shall make your count for the lamb. Your lamb shall be without blemish, a male of the first year. You may take it from the sheep or from the goats. Now you shall keep it until the fourteenth day of the same month. Then the whole assembly of the congregation of Israel shall kill it at twilight. And they shall take some of the blood and put it on the two doorposts and on the lintel of the houses where they eat it. Then they shall eat the flesh on that night; roasted in fire, with unleavened bread*

and with bitter herbs they shall eat it. Do not eat it raw, nor boiled at all with water, but roasted in fire — its head with its legs and its entrails. You shall let none of it remain until morning, and what remains of it until morning you shall burn with fire. And thus you shall eat it: with a belt on your waist, your sandals on your feet, and your staff in your hand. So you shall eat it in haste. It is the LORD's Passover.'"

— Exodus 12:1–11

Then Moses called for all the elders of Israel and said to them, "Pick out and take lambs for yourselves according to your families, and kill the Passover lamb. And you shall take a bunch of hyssop, dip it in the blood that is in the basin, and strike the lintel and the two doorposts with the blood that is in the basin. And none of you shall go out of the door of his house until morning. For the LORD will pass through to strike the Egyptians; and when He sees the blood on the lintel and on the two doorposts, the LORD will pass over the door and not allow the destroyer to come into your houses to strike you. And you shall observe this thing as an ordinance for you and your sons forever."

— Exodus 12:21–24

Consider how much the world has changed and what events have taken place during the last one thousand years. Yet well over one thousand years after the first Passover lamb was killed, four days before Passover, the Lamb of God came down from the Mount of Olives with great celebration. John the Baptist had already called Messiah Yeshua the Lamb of God who takes away the sins of the world.

> *The next day John saw Jesus coming toward him, and said, "Behold! The Lamb of God who takes away the sin of the world!"*
>
> — John 1:29

During this one moment of His entering Jerusalem, along with fulfilling the Passover, we also see Messiah Yeshua fulfilling Bible Prophecy from the prophets Nathan and then Zechariah (written in 400s BC). Additionally, we see previews of the fulfillment of the David Covenant. After the passing of so many centuries since this was all predicted, we also learn that David is another father of our faith. In this snapshot of time, so much is happening. Look and see:

> *Rejoice greatly, O daughter of Zion! Shout, O daughter of Jerusalem!*
> *Behold, your King is coming to you He is just and having salvation, Lowly and riding on a donkey,*
> *A colt, the foal of a donkey.*
>
> — Zechariah 9:9

> *Then they brought the colt to Jesus and threw their clothes on it, and He sat on it. And many spread their clothes on the road, and others cut down leafy branches from the trees and spread them on the road. Then those who went before and those who followed cried out, saying:*

"Hosanna!
Blessed is He who comes in the name of the Lord!
Blessed is the kingdom of our father David
That comes in the name of the Lord! Hosanna in
the highest!"

And Jesus went into Jerusalem and into the temple. So
when He had looked around at all things, as the hour
was already late, He went out to Bethany with the
twelve.

— Mark 11:7–11,
written in the first century AD

They cry out "Hosanna," which means "save us," and is also used as "glory in the highest," to the King on a donkey, Who is the Son of David and the Lamb of God. He comes into the Holy City at Passover season, and during the four days leading up to the slaughter of Passover lambs in Jerusalem, the religious leaders try to find blemishes in "The Lamb":

Then they asked Him, saying, "Teacher, we know
that You say and teach rightly, and You do not show
personal favoritism,
but teach the way of God in truth: Is it lawful for
us to pay taxes to Caesar or not?"
But He perceived their craftiness, and said to
them, "Why do you test Me? Show Me a denarius.
Whose image and inscription does it have?"
They answered and said, "Caesar's."

And He said to them, "Render therefore to Caesar
the things that are Caesar's, and to God the things
that are God's."

— Luke 20:21–25

The religious leaders continue to try and find blemishes in the sinless Lamb, asking Him more "gotcha" questions. Each time, they come up empty because they are speaking to the only begotten Son of God. He is the One who created everything, including them!

The Lamb presents the most important Passover ceremony in history. The traditional name for the ceremony is "seder," which means "order." Remember, the first Passover culminated in the Moses Covenant. What is the sign of the Passover and later, the Moses Covenant? It is the blood:

Now the blood shall be a sign for you on the houses
where you are. And when I see the blood, I will pass
over you; and the plague shall not be on you to destroy
you when I strike the land of Egypt.

— Exodus 12:13

So Moses came and told the people all the words of
the LORD and all the judgments. And all the peo-
ple answered with one voice and said, "All the words
which the LORD has said we will do." And Moses
wrote all the words of the LORD. And he rose early
in the morning, and built an altar at the foot of the
mountain, and twelve pillars according to the twelve
tribes of Israel. Then he sent young men of the children

of Israel, who offered burnt offerings and sacrificed
peace offerings of oxen to the LORD. And Moses took
half the blood and put it in basins, and half the blood
he sprinkled on the altar. Then he took the Book of the
Covenant and read in the hearing of the people. And
they said, "All that the LORD has said we will do,
and be obedient." And Moses took the blood, sprinkled
it on the people, and said, "This is the blood of the cov-
enant which the LORD has made with you according
to all these words."

— Exodus 24:3–8

We have seen the blood of the Passover Lamb and the blood of the Moses Covenant. Then we heard John the Baptist's announcement and the people of Israel crying out Hosanna to the Son of David riding down the Mount of Olives on a donkey, just as Zechariah foretold. Now, let's join the Passover where the Lamb of God is at the center of the seder.

The Jewish disciples of Messiah Jesus are laying or reclining at the table, which is ordered to tell the story of the deliverance from the bondage of Egypt. On the table are four cups of wine. The Lamb picks up the cup called "The Cup of Redemption."

Then He took the cup, and gave thanks, and gave it
to them, saying, "Drink from it, all of you. For this is
My blood of the new covenant, which is shed for many
for the remission of sins.

— Matthew 26:27–28

It was the blood of lambs that redeemed the children of Israel from their slavery in Egypt. Now, it is the blood of the Lamb Messiah Yeshua that will make deliverance available — not only for the children of Israel, but for the entire world. And this time, the redemption is not deliverance from a wicked Pharaoh, but from Satan, death, sin, and the grave.

In Egypt, the blood of lambs on the sides and above the doorposts saved Israel from the wrath of God. But now it is the blood of the Lamb Messiah Jesus, who was lifted up between two thieves — when applied to the doorpost of any sinner's heart — that provides forgiveness of every sin and saves us from the wrath of God. Through the blood of "The Lamb," every sinner — Jew and Gentile — can spend this life and the life to come with our great Creator Abba Father, Son Messiah Yeshua, and the Holy Spirit. And through what vehicle are these grand and glorious things accomplished? THE NEW COVENANT!

> *For God so loved the world that He gave His only begotten Son, that whoever believes in Him should not perish but have everlasting life.*
> — John 3:16

Then, as lambs are being sacrificed at the assigned place at the Temple in Jerusalem, "The" Passover Lamb, bloody and beaten, goes up onto the cross. His mission accomplished, the Lamb proclaims three words of victory:

> *Now a vessel full of sour wine was sitting there; and they filled a sponge with sour wine, put it on hyssop,*

and put it to His mouth. So when Jesus had received
the sour wine, He said, "It is finished!" And bowing
His head, He gave up His spirit.

— John 19:29–30

In Israel during that time, the New Testament Greek expression that is usually translated into English as "it is finished" was also a way to say "paid in full." That expression would have been written on a legal document proving a debt was paid. In some cases, it would have been nailed to the front door of a home. The sinless Lamb of God was nailed to the cross, paying all our sin debt. Those who receive Yeshua as Lord receive the benefit of this full payment. There is a New Covenant passage written by Paul the apostle that says this so well:

And you, being dead in your trespasses and the un-
circumcision of your flesh, He has made alive together
with Him, having forgiven you all trespasses, having
wiped out the handwriting of requirements that was
against us, which was contrary to us. And He has
taken it out of the way, having nailed it to the cross.

— Colossians 2:13,14

Then, on the third day after the Lamb of God died — Hallelujah — He rose from the grave. Now the Lamb of God is in heaven and is the only One worthy to unfold the rest of the story. During the time of the soon-to-come tribulation on earth, songs will be sung in heaven. One of them is the Song of Moses, which marks the celebration of the triumph over

Pharaoh's army. Another is called the Song of the Lamb; here is part of it:

> *They sing the song of Moses, the servant of God, and the song of the Lamb, saying:*
> *"Great and marvelous are Your works, Lord God Almighty!*
> *Just and true are Your ways,*
> *O King of the saints!"*
>
> — Revelation 15:3

There is much to tell about the Lamb of God, but for now, remember this is simply one of many examples of the marvelous and majestic power of the LORD God — Father, Son, and Holy Spirit — as He brings forth the New Covenant. He makes His covenant promises and unfolds them through His prophetic word, which is working in the earth. In terms of revelation and knowledge of the Holy God of Heaven, Paul had more than most. Maybe he said it best in the New Covenant book of Romans:

> *Oh, the depth of the riches both of the wisdom and knowledge of God!*
> *How unsearchable are His judgments and His ways past finding out!*
> *"For who has known the mind of the Lord? Or who has become His counselor?"*
> *"Or who has first given to Him*
> *And it shall be repaid to him?"*
>
> — Romans 11:33–35

CHAPTER 4

Where Do I Fit In?

*For I am not ashamed of the gospel of Christ, for it
is the power of God to salvation for everyone who
believes...*

— Romans 1:16a

Having read this far, some Christians may be wondering why they have never heard some of this. It may seem strange to hear that such important matters pertaining to our faith sound so Jewish and Israeli. These are things not generally discussed in modern theology or in most churches. While some fragments are common knowledge in church, they are not often a focus or priority.

There is also a question a non-Jewish believer in Messiah Jesus might be asking at this point: where do I fit in? Great question — and what a plan Elohim has for an answer! As a matter of fact, the Bible passage that ended the last chapter was really an exclamation of how the Lord unfolds His New Covenant plans for both Jews and Gentiles. Both are equally in need of His grace and mercy. By the way, that is Bible Prophecy.

Please stay with me, as this plan is so exciting for every believer in Messiah Yeshua. If you embrace these powerful truths for your life and anticipate their unfolding in this special prophetic generation — wow, what a life you will live! My humble prayer is that through the rest of the chapters of this book, just a glimpse of what is in store for this generation of watching and ready believers in Messiah Jesus will be effectively conveyed.

Most importantly, all Jews and Gentiles fit into the plan of Elohim — the Father, Son, and Holy Spirit — because God loves all equally. The place where we all fit is in the heart of Abba Father. He loves everyone so much that He sent His only begotten Son to give His life to save us. Paul the apostle explains how this plan of love unfolds through the Lord's covenant with the people of Israel to all nations.

In his letter to the first-century Roman believers (not to be confused with Roman Catholicism, which did not exist at this time), Paul explains the new relationship between Jews and Gentiles who believe in Messiah.

We have learned, and will further explore, some of the reasons the Lord cast the Jewish people out of Israel, scattering them to the far corners of the world. Sadly, too few non-Jewish believers have considered one significant purpose for this. Could it be so that the Gentiles who are being saved could then share the gospel with the Jewish people who live all around them? Here is a great idea — the Gentiles should be so incredibly thankful to have the Jew's Messiah that they provoke some of the Jewish people to jealousy so that they also want to be saved. After all, the gospel went to the nations because of the Jews rejecting it. That being said, the Lord earnestly wants to save them.

Brethren, my heart's desire and prayer to God for Israel is that they may be saved.

— Romans 10:1

I say then, have they stumbled that they should fall? Certainly not! But through their fall, to provoke them to jealousy, salvation has come to the Gentiles. Now if their fall is riches for the world, and their failure riches for the Gentiles, how much more their fullness! For I speak to you Gentiles; inasmuch as I am an apostle to the Gentiles, I magnify my ministry, if by any means I may provoke to jealousy those who are my flesh and save some of them. For if their being cast away is the reconciling of the world, what will their acceptance be but life from the dead?

— Romans 11:11–15

Paul then writes about two olive trees — one a cultivated tree (the Jews) and the other a wild olive tree (the Gentiles). Many of the branches from the Jewish tree break off and fall to the ground — representing unbelief in Messiah Jesus. Some of the branches from the Gentile tree are then taken and grafted onto the Jewish tree of faith. The roots of the Jewish tree are the covenants Elohim made with the fathers Abraham, Isaac, and Israel, including the New Covenant. He teaches that Gentile believers had better heed the warning not to be arrogant against unbelieving Israel. Wouldn't it be better to participate in the plan instead of being indifferent or working against it?

*For if the firstfruit is holy, the lump is also holy; and if
the root is holy, so are the branches. And if some of the
branches were broken off, and you, being a wild olive
tree, were grafted in among them, and with them
became a partaker of the root and fatness of the olive
tree, do not boast against the branches. But if you do
boast, remember that you do not support the root, but
the root supports you.*

*You will say then, "Branches were broken off that
I might be grafted in." Well said. Because of unbelief they were broken off, and you stand by faith. Do
not be haughty, but fear. For if God did not spare
the natural branches, He may not spare you either.
Therefore consider the goodness and severity of God:
on those who fell, severity; but toward you, goodness,
if you continue in His goodness. Otherwise you also
will be cut off. And they also, if they do not continue
in unbelief, will be grafted in, for God is able to graft
them in again. For if you were cut out of the olive tree
which is wild by nature, and were grafted contrary
to nature into a cultivated olive tree, how much more
will these, who are natural branches, be grafted into
their own olive tree?*

— Romans 11:16–24

After almost two thousand years, why have so many
non-Jewish Christians never considered these things? It is for
the same reason that the worst persecutors of Jews through the
centuries have not been Muslims, but Christians. You might
say, "Oh, but they could not have been real Christians like to-

day." Due to the purpose of this book and the need to stay on track, I will not be able to go more deeply into this matter.

Many would shudder if they knew today's big-name church leaders who are indifferent and even against the Lord's prophetic plans in this hour because of their views regarding Israel. The same could be said of the so-called "Church Fathers." Remember, and this will help you at this time more than ever — the real Church Fathers are Abraham, Isaac, and Jacob.

Through the centuries, many of the so-called Church Fathers and their disciples, right up to today, hate(d) the Jewish people. You do not have to look far to find this information, and it is horribly ugly — just go to any internet search engine. This hate necessitated, and today necessitates, changing our faith and reconfiguring Bible Prophecy because Israel is central to our faith due to the Lord's covenants and His prophetic word. Remember, He is the God of Israel. There are powerful Bible passages that instruct and help keep us from being misled:

> *For I do not desire, brethren, that you should be ig-*
> *norant of this mystery, lest you should be wise in your*
> *own opinion, that blindness in part has happened to*
> *Israel until the fullness of the Gentiles has come in.*
> *And so all Israel will be saved, as it is written:*
> *"The Deliverer will come out of Zion,*
> *And He will turn away ungodliness from Jacob;*
> *For this is My covenant with them,*
> *When I take away their sins."*
> — Romans 11:25–27

Tragically, the warning to not be arrogant against unbelieving Israel has been ignored by so many Christians. There is a partial blindness over the eyes of the Jewish people that will be removed at the coming of Messiah Yeshua. All of Israel who is alive at the time of the coming of the Lord will be saved. Today is the time of the Gentiles; then it will be the Day of The Lord. Yet there has always been a plan in place to get the gospel to the Jews who will be saved and the nations. This plan necessitates Gentile believers loving the Jews.

Our Creator has designated an order for the gospel to go out to the world. That order has been largely ignored for almost two thousand years; but I am a witness that if one who is born again walks in this order, it brings an entirely new and exciting dimension to life. I know some non-Jewish believers who do this, and they are anything but boring. So, here it is:

> *For I am not ashamed of the gospel of Christ, for it is the power of God to salvation for everyone who believes, for the Jew first and also for the Greek.*
> — Romans 1:16

Back then, the word "Greek" in this context meant non-Jewish or Gentile. Does this passage say that the gospel used to be to the Jew first and this has changed? Does it say that the gospel used to be to the Jew first but now it is just for the Gentile? Is the gospel still the power of God to provide salvation for everyone who believes? Is that still true for today? Of course it is, so unless you monkey with Bible grammar, the gospel is still to the Jew first.

Interestingly, I read in one of his biographies that the renowned great man of faith George Mueller started his ministry by taking the gospel to Jewish people in London. It has been said that Hudson Taylor, the great missionary to China, began each year by sending a check to the Jewish Bishop Michael Solomon Alexander in Jerusalem. In the memo section, he would write: "to the Jew first." Later in the year, a check would come to Hudson Taylor from Jerusalem that would say something to the effect of "and then to the Gentiles."

The way predominantly Gentile churches, with a sprinkling of Jews, fit into the plan is that we are to be salt and light to a lost and dying world as one new man in Messiah Yeshua (Ephesians 2:15). We are to be authentic disciples of Messiah Yeshua. We are to be taking the gospel to the nations and making disciples. We are to do so in His order because of His covenants with Israel.

Remember, it is for the sake of those in the nations who need salvation that the Jewish people have such a sharp enmity toward the gospel. And yes, I will prove that with Scripture. It is all the plan of the Lord, yet the Jewish people are beloved of God for the sake of the Church Fathers: Abraham, Isaac, and Israel.

Concerning the gospel they are enemies for your sake,
but concerning the election they are beloved for the
sake of the fathers. For the gifts and the calling of
God are irrevocable. For as you were once disobedient
to God, yet have now obtained mercy through their
disobedience, even so these also have now been dis-
obedient, that through the mercy shown you they also

may obtain mercy. For God has committed them all to
disobedience, that He might have mercy on all.

— Romans 11:28–32

What if I told you that every non-Jewish follower of Messiah Jesus is a walking, talking, breathing fulfillment of covenant and Bible Prophecy? Just waking up every day being forgiven for sin, loving Messiah Jesus, and living for Him presents the world with a witness that the Holy One of Israel keeps His promises? Remember the seventh promise of the Abraham Covenant?

And in you all the families of the earth shall be blessed.

— Genesis 12:3

As believers in Messiah Yeshua, we are His beloved children, whom He has called to give Him glory and worship Him in spirit and in truth. This generation of born-again believers has been given a special assignment. As we transition from covenant to prophecy, know this: any follower of Messiah Yeshua who will let these covenant truths be a foundation for their understanding of what is coming will live out a life that no other generation possibly could — starting now!

CHAPTER 5

Israel's Labor Pains

Who has heard such a thing?

— Isaiah 66:8

The Scatterings and Gatherings

No matter what man says or does, the word of God will be found true. This is because Messiah Yeshua is the way, the truth, and the life. So it is regarding the scattering of the Jewish people to the nations of the world. His word is true, and they have been scattered for thousands of years.

The primary early scatterings took place at the hand of these empires:

- 722 BC: Assyrian invasion — the ten northern tribes of Israel were scattered.
- 605–586 BC: Babylonian siege — waves of Israelis living in the southern kingdom of Judah were taken captive to Babylon.

The Babylonian captivity included prophetic promises, some written by Isaiah well over one hundred years earlier that declared the Jewish captives would return to Jerusalem. One of the most significant prophecies was from Jeremiah, who predicted with exact timing when the Jews would return. These promises were kept right on time because, as the song goes, "He's an on-time God!"

> *For thus says the LORD: After seventy years are*
> *completed at Babylon, I will visit you and perform*
> *My good word toward you, and cause you to return to*
> *this place.*
>
> *— Jeremiah 29:10*

While the Jews were in Babylon, just as the LORD promised well over one hundred years earlier, He raised up King Cyrus of Persia to conquer Babylon. Then our great Creator showed Cyrus why he had become such a powerful ruler. Cyrus could not deny Bible Prophecy.

> *Who says of Cyrus, "He is My shepherd, And he shall*
> *perform all My pleasure, Saying to Jerusalem, 'You*
> *shall be built,' And to the temple, 'Your foundation*
> *shall be laid.'"*
>
> *— Isaiah 44:28*

> *Now in the first year of Cyrus king of Persia, that the*
> *word of the LORD by the mouth of Jeremiah might be*
> *fulfilled, the LORD stirred up the spirit of Cyrus king*
> *of Persia, so that he made a proclamation throughout*
> *all his kingdom, and also put it in writing, saying;*
> *Thus says Cyrus king of Persia:*

All the kingdoms of the earth the LORD God of heaven has given me. And He has commanded me to build Him a house at Jerusalem which is in Judah. Who is among you of all His people? May the LORD his God be with him, and let him go up!

— 2 Chronicles 36:22–23

Let's stop for a moment and consider a few things. King Cyrus worshipped gods foreign to those of the Elohim of Israel. This man is the most powerful king on the planet, yet he harnesses the resources at his disposal to send the Jews back to Jerusalem right at seventy years, according to Bible Prophecy.

There are two reasons why Cyrus did that, and I will give them in the proper order. The first reason is that, just as Isaiah 46:9–11 says regarding Cyrus, the Elohim of Israel does whatever He wants, whenever He wants, using whomever He wants. The second reason is that Cyrus is no dummy. Even though he and the LORD have never met before, because of the awesome nature of Bible Prophecy, Cyrus cannot deny who the real KING is.

You see, it would be absolutely foolish and insane to deny that only the true and living God could so long beforehand predict that Cyrus's kingdom would overtake Babylon and even mention him by name. King Cyrus knew his was an assigned position in his generation. Understanding Bible Prophecy, Cyrus knew that Elohim had raised him up for exclusively powerful works. Sadly, so many believers in this same Lord of Israel don't understand as much as this pagan king. But for those who do, boy, are we in for an exciting ride!

Here is a word for all who love Messiah Jesus and grab hold of it:

For we are His workmanship, created in Christ Jesus for good works, which God prepared beforehand that we should walk in them.

— Ephesians 2:10

Having been brought back to their land by the promise-keeping LORD, the Jewish people dwelt in Israel through many ups and downs. Then, in 70 AD and about 135 AD, those who survived the Roman onslaughts were expelled from Jerusalem and northern Israel. Many were taken to Rome as slaves and scattered throughout the earth.

The Jewish people have been misunderstood, hated, and horribly mistreated all over the earth down through the centuries. The promises Moses prophesied in the Torah (first five books of the Bible) have tragically come true. However, just because the LORD uses the wickedness in men's hearts to dispense discipline, judgment, and even wrath, that does not mean the Jew-haters are in the clear. On the contrary, the LORD has judged, is judging, and will judge those who were His instruments of justice. They are assigned deserved punishment for mistreating the Jew, even if they were acting as a tool in His hands. This is clearly demonstrated through the prophetic word of Elohim and will continue to unfold in the pages ahead.

In the midst of all this heartache and tragedy, the Bible prophets have much to say about the end of this age and the gathering of the Jewish people back in the land of Israel. In the

1600s, things began to change in the hearts of a handful of believers in Messiah Jesus in England. While Jewish people were being kicked around in other European countries, a process often instigated by church leaders, a warmth began to soften the hearts of this English remnant. This warmth became a flicker and then a flame as sweeping revivals took place.

This spread to the colonies and, of course, what became the United States, as regional revivals took place in America. Interestingly, along with this love of Messiah and affection for His first-born son, two radical shifts set the world stage for Bible Prophecy to blossom. England, and later America, became world powers at the same time they were supportive of the Jewish people and their return to their homeland. In the fifth chapter of my book *America's Ark*, I write about some of these details for those interested in more puzzle pieces.

In the late 1800s, an Austrian Jewish journalist named Theodore Herzl was significantly impacted by the Dreyfus affair in France and caught the vision for the Jewish people returning to their homeland. The Dreyfus affair involved a trumped-up charge against a Jewish French officer that fueled another ugly wave of persecution against the Jews. Herzl had a great deal of influence and support from British and American Christian leaders. This was the beginning of the Zionist movement — Hallelujah!

A wave of Jewish immigration from Europe began taking place at that time. Many of them went to a haven of relatively peaceful coexistence and opportunity: the USA. While a steady trickle began to water the arid Promised Land, they flooded the hearts of those who taught and knew Bible Prophecy. Finally, after so many years, the fuse of the end-times prophetic scenarios had been lit.

For me to say such a thing would be irresponsible and reckless if the Word of God was not very clear about the matter. There is a valuable resource that our Father in heaven has given us to understand the times and seasons. It sits mostly untapped, ready to pour into our hearts, minds, and lives to prepare us for this hour.

The Prophets and the Prophetic Word

Somehow, many Christians think that with the coming of the New Covenant, the Old Testament prophets' writings are unimportant and were already completely fulfilled. This is the opposite of the truth. The words of the prophets that rightly predicted the manner in which Messiah Jesus would come the first time also rightly predict, with great detail, end-time prophetic scenarios that will usher in His return.

If you remember what we learned together in the covenant chapters, you know that those end-times scenarios revolve around the land and people of Israel, because He is the Elohim of Israel and made promises to Abraham, Isaac, and the man named Israel.

> *He is the LORD our God;*
>> *His judgments are in all the earth. He remembers*
> *His covenant forever,*
>> *The word which He commanded, for a thousand*
> *generations, The covenant which He made with*
> *Abraham,*
>> *And His oath to Isaac,*

And confirmed it to Jacob for a statute, To Israel as an everlasting covenant,

Saying, "To you I will give the land of Canaan As the allotment of your inheritance,"

When they were few in number,

Indeed very few, and strangers in it.

— Psalm 105:7–12

From the late 1800s to the early 1900s, this steady trickle of Jews continued streaming into the Promised Land. They overcame impossible (but for Elohim) obstacles. The areas in Israel with water were uninhabitable marshes teeming with malaria, and the rest was barren mountains, wilderness, and desert. Only by the grace and mercy of the Lord were they able to inhabit this uninhabitable land. Then something miraculous began to happen — it is not that it was *like* the land began to live — it did begin to live.

And you, son of man, prophesy to the mountains of Israel, and say, "O mountains of Israel, hear the word of the LORD! Thus says the Lord God: 'Because the enemy has said of you, "Aha! The ancient heights have become our possession,"' therefore prophesy, and say, "Thus says the Lord God: 'Because they made you desolate and swallowed you up on every side, so that you became the possession of the rest of the nations, and you are taken up by the lips of talkers and slandered by the people' — therefore, O mountains of Israel, hear the word of the Lord God! Thus says the Lord God to the mountains, the hills, the rivers, the valleys, the

desolate wastes, and the cities that have been forsaken,
which became plunder and mockery to the rest of the
nations all around — therefore thus says the Lord
God: 'Surely I have spoken in My burning jealousy
against the rest of the nations and against all Edom,
who gave My land to themselves as a possession, with
wholehearted joy and spiteful minds, in order to plun-
der its open country.'"

Therefore prophesy concerning the land of Israel,
and say to the mountains, the hills, the rivers, and
the valleys, "Thus says the Lord God: "Behold, I have
spoken in My jealousy and My fury, because you have
borne the shame of the nations.' Therefore thus says the
Lord God: "I have raised My hand in an oath that
surely the nations that are around you shall bear their
own shame. But you, O mountains of Israel, you shall
shoot forth your branches and yield your fruit to My
people Israel, for they are about to come. For indeed
I am for you, and I will turn to you, and you shall
be tilled and sown. I will multiply men upon you,
all the house of Israel, all of it; and the cities shall be
inhabited and the ruins rebuilt. I will multiply upon
you man and beast; and they shall increase and bear
young; I will make you inhabited as in former times,
and do better for you than at your beginnings. Then
you shall know that I am the LORD."

— Ezekiel 36:1–11

During World Wars I and II, the stream of Jewish immigration to the Promised Land became broader and deeper. The

violent shaking associated with these catastrophic wars pushed the Jews back to their homeland. This was especially the case in World War II as the persecution against the Jews in Europe ramped up and added swelling to the stream, turning it into a river. This was no accident — this was the Elohim of Israel and His prophetic word. It has been said that the First World War prepared the land for the Jews while the Second World War prepared the Jews for the land.

In 1917, Lord Balfour, a British statesman, issued the famous Balfour Declaration, giving great backing to the creation of a Jewish state in the Promised Land. The British, for hundreds of years, had been instrumental in sending the Jews back to their land and later issued the McDonald White Paper in 1939, thus cementing England's 180-degree turn from Zionism and support for a Jewish homeland. Tragically, as they wielded great political and military influence through their Middle East Mandate from World War I, they turned Jews fleeing to the land back into Hitler's clutches. This was portrayed in the 1976 film, *Voyage of the Damned*.

By doing so, England sealed her fate and precipitated her exit from the world stage in terms of their previous world power position. Shortly after sending the Jews back to the murderous hands of Hitler — London began experiencing the German monster's Luftwaffe. Where it was once said "the sun never sets on the British empire," England is now a shadow of her former self. The Abrahamic curse is alive and well. Thankfully, there is still a vibrant remnant of the old English who love the Jewish people and the land of Israel. I personally know many of them.

Israel's Birth

With one exception, never has a nation lost its people to war, had its people cast out of that land, and then later had their descendants, having maintained their nationality without assimilation, reclaim that land and nation. Additionally, it has never happened that, while reclaiming that nation, those descendants revived their ancient language and culture including their ancient currency — shekels. Of course, these are all prophetic fulfillments of the covenant nation Israel. And Israel has done this not once, but twice: after the Babylonian exile and now. For almost two thousand years, there was no Israel on the map, and then came the rebirth.

Isaiah the prophet gives us one of those mountaintop prophecies I mentioned earlier. He writes of a time and events that unmistakably mark the physical rebirth, and then the spiritual birth, of the covenant land and people of Israel. One very important thing to remember about birth is that it comes after intense labor pains.

Before sharing the verses, I have to ask what may seem a silly question: When does an expectant mother experience labor pains — before or after the birth of the baby? I told you the question may seem silly, and of course, the answer is before the baby is born — but these are very unique labor pains that result in a very unique birth.

"Before she was in labor, she gave birth; Before her pain came,
  She delivered a male child. Who has heard such a thing? Who has seen such things?

Shall the earth be made to give birth in one day?
Or shall a nation be born at once?
For as soon as Zion was in labor, She gave birth
to her children.
Shall I bring to the time of birth, and not cause
delivery?" says the LORD. "Shall I who cause delivery
shut up the womb?" says your God.

— Isaiah 66:7–9

Let's unpack this passage together. Isaiah speaks of two births that obviously would have two different times of labor. Isaiah's focus for this passage is a future labor after a male child is born. Who is the mother, and who is the male child, and when do the earlier labor pains take place? If we can understand that, we can move on to the later labor pains.

Thankfully, we have the word of the living God of Israel, Who has revealed the answer to these questions. The New Covenant book of Revelation explains who the mother is through an incident that took place in the book of Genesis. You may remember that Joseph had two God-given dreams, and we will look at the second one.

Then he dreamed still another dream and told it to
his brothers, and said, "Look, I have dreamed another
dream. And this time, the sun, the moon, and the elev-
en stars bowed down to me."
So he told it to his father and his brothers; and
his father rebuked him and said to him, "What is this
dream that you have dreamed? Shall your mother and

I and your brothers indeed come to bow down to the
earth before you?"

— Genesis 37:9–10

In this dream, Israel is the sun, Rachel is the moon, and Israel's sons are the stars. All we have to do is let the Bible interpret itself. We then can know who the expecting mother is in Isaiah's mysterious chapter 66.

Now a great sign appeared in heaven: a woman
clothed with the sun, with the moon under her feet,
and on her head a garland of twelve stars. Then being
with child, she cried out in labor and in pain to give
birth.

— Revelation 12:1–2

This woman has been interpreted as many things — an internet search will harvest many possibilities. But if you know your Bible, you understand that the passage must be interpreted in light of Genesis 37, which says this is Israel. The context of Revelation 12 will help us confirm it. We will also clearly learn who the male child from Isaiah 66 is as well.

And another sign appeared in heaven: behold, a great,
fiery red dragon having seven heads and ten horns,
and seven diadems on his heads. His tail drew a third
of the stars of heaven and threw them to the earth.
And the dragon stood before the woman who was
ready to give birth, to devour her Child as soon as it
was born. She bore a male Child who was to rule all

nations with a rod of iron. And her Child was caught
up to God and His throne.

— Revelation 12:3–5

Remember, these things in Revelation 12 are signs that point to something. There is a point to all of this. Our King Messiah Yeshua wants us to see the signs and live with understanding.

A fierce dragon with seven heads and ten horns refers to the final world empire before the second coming of Messiah Jesus mentioned in Daniel 7. The dragon deceives and corrupts one-third of the Lord's angels. We know from the gospel account in Matthew that this dragon also deceived King Herod into trying to kill Messiah Jesus after His birth into this earth. We know from Acts 1, Revelation 3, and Psalm 2 that after His resurrection and having been with our Father in heaven, King Messiah Jesus will return to rule the world with a rod of iron. See, it is not so mysterious if you know your Bible!

This fiery red dragon is identified as Satan:

And war broke out in heaven: Michael and his angels
fought with the dragon; and the dragon and his angels
fought, but they did not prevail, nor was a place found
for them in heaven any longer. So the great dragon
was cast out, that serpent of old, called the Devil and
Satan, who deceives the whole world; he was cast to
the earth, and his angels were cast out with him.

— Revelation 12:7–9

So then, we know the expecting mother is Israel and the male child is Messiah Yeshua. Isaiah and Revelation speak of labor pains as Israel births Yeshua into the earth. These are the early birth pains I mentioned. Yet clearly, Isaiah speaks of later birth pains. Are they also mentioned in Revelation 12?

The answer is *yes*. Often, the prophets would write about two or more events in a short passage of Scripture. What they did not know is that there may be thousands of years between those events. Here is an example:

> *Rejoice greatly, O daughter of Zion! Shout, O daughter of Jerusalem!*
>
> *Behold, your King is coming to you; He is just and having salvation, Lowly and riding on a donkey, A colt, the foal of a donkey.*
>
> *I will cut off the chariot from Ephraim And the horse from Jerusalem;*
>
> *The battle bow shall be cut off.*
>
> *He shall speak peace to the nations; His dominion shall be from sea to sea,*
>
> *And from the River to the ends of the earth.*
>
> — Zechariah 9:9–10

Bible Prophecy declares that King Messiah will come lowly and riding on a donkey, but also that He will reign as the world's King. What that passage does not tell you is that the period at the end of one sentence separates the next sentence by nearly two thousand years. It is the same with the woman's birth pains in Revelation 12.

Israel's early pains, which are associated with the birth of Messiah Jesus, are separated by about two thousand years from the later labor pains. Messiah Jesus spoke of a time that will be the world's great tribulation. The second half of that time is repeatedly identified as three and a half years. With no mention of a time gap, Revelation 12 jumps ahead from the birth of Messiah Jesus to speaking of the end of Israel's later labor pains.

> *She bore a male Child who was to rule all nations with a rod of iron. And her Child was caught up to God and His throne. Then the woman fled into the wilderness, where she has a place prepared by God, that they should feed her there one thousand two hundred and sixty days.*
> — Revelation 12:5–6

Now we know who the woman is, who the male child is, and that Israel's later birth pains lead to the second coming of Messiah Jesus sitting on the throne of David. Now back to Isaiah 66.

> *"Before she was in labor, she gave birth; Before her pain came,*
> *She delivered a male child. Who has heard such a thing? Who has seen such things?*
> *Shall the earth be made to give birth in one day? Or shall a nation be born at once?*
> *For as soon as Zion was in labor, She gave birth to her children.*

Shall I bring to the time of birth, and not cause
delivery?" says the LORD. "Shall I who cause delivery
shut up the womb?" says your God.

— Isaiah 66:7–9

These are rhetorical questions, and the answer to the two pertaining to the sudden physical rebirth of Israel is clearly — YES! The earth can be made to give birth in one day, and we know that because the word "for" is used when referring to those questions. Furthermore, Israel is once again referred to as the mother in labor, and beyond that — in the heart of Elohim — this futuristic event Isaiah writes of has already taken place in the mind and heart of the Lord. It is so important to understand that Elohim is able to make the future take place before it happens because He is not limited by time. He has already made and seen it happen.

Again, what is it that He has made and seen happen beforehand? It is Zion, the land of Israel, giving physical birth to the children of a man named Israel. Amazingly, that which was futuristic to Isaiah we have seen fulfilled. On May 14, 1948, in one day, the world saw Isaiah 66 burst from the pages of the Bible into this generation. The covenant nation of Genesis 12 was suddenly thrust back on the world scene. This is not the end but only the beginning of Israel's birth pains. The reason is that the baby is not yet fully birthed. The Isaiah passage continues:

"Shall I bring to the time of birth, and not cause delivery?" says the LORD. "Shall I who cause delivery shut up the womb?" says your God.

— Isaiah 66:9

The Lord God of Israel is saying there will be a time He has designated to bring Israel to full-term birth. Just as with a woman in labor, the frequency and intensity of the birth pains will increase. And we see from this Isaiah passage that there will be a two-stage birthing process — a time of birth and delivery. In other words, this verse is saying that the LORD who brought Israel to physical birth will also bring Israel to spiritual birth.

Often while in Africa or other places teaching Bible Prophecy, I share the percentages of Israelis who have not yet believed in Messiah Yeshua. People are astonished that at the time of this writing, approximately 99.7 percent of Israelis do not believe in Messiah Yeshua. Generally speaking, here is their question; since Israel is at the center of so much prophetic fulfillment: "How can it be that the People of the Book do not believe in the Messiah of the Book?"

I want to say, "How can so many Christians, while the Bible is leaping off the pages, not understand the Lord's program with Israel?" However, this is not how I respond as there is a more graceful answer. There are so many clear prophecies in the Bible that explain the Lord's prophetic plan: there is a large contingency of the Jewish people He has designated to bring back from the nations to the Promised Land, and then He will bring them to the spiritual birth.

For I will take you from among the nations, gather
you out of all countries, and bring you into your own
land. Then I will sprinkle clean water on you, and you
shall be clean; I will cleanse you from all your filth-
iness and from all your idols. I will give you a new
heart and put a new spirit within you; I will take the
heart of stone out of your flesh and give you a heart of
flesh.

I will put My Spirit within you and cause you to
walk in My statutes, and you will keep My judgments
and do them. Then you shall dwell in the land that
I gave to your fathers; you shall be My people, and I
will be your God.

— Ezekiel 36:24–28

The prophet Ezekiel tells us that the Ruach HaKodesh (Holy Spirit) will first bring the children of Israel into their own land and then, afterward, bring them to spiritual birth. Israel's labor pains have brought forth the physical birth of their nation. Yet the Holy One of Israel has planned very specific scenarios to bring them to a place where they will cry out to Messiah Jesus to save them — which He will!

CHAPTER 6

The Nations Join the Labor Party

All these are the beginning of sorrows.
— Matthew 24:8

In the previous chapter, the Isaiah passage speaks of how the physical and spiritual birth of Israel is marked with labor pains. Much of that labor is at the hands of the nations as they resist the Holy One of Israel and declare war on Him and His covenants. However, not to worry — it is all part of His plan. You see, the LORD is a man of war!

The LORD is a man of war; the LORD is His name.
— Exodus 15:3

These are the victorious words proclaimed by Moses and the children of Israel after the LORD made short work of the world's mightiest army — Egypt. Today the world is behaving the same way as it increasingly unifies against the Holy One of Israel. Truly, the nations have joined the labor party!

Three of the New Covenant Gospel accounts have similar earthshaking prophetic scenarios. Matthew 24, Mark 13, and Luke 21 have some variations, yet they dovetail perfectly as they answer some of the most important questions ever asked.

Let's start at the end of Matthew 23, with the reminder that originally there were no chapter breaks in the Bible. Our Messiah Yeshua is speaking with His disciples about the judgment that will come to Jerusalem. His heart is so heavy, as He has loved this city and its inhabitants for thousands of years while mostly receiving back hatred and mocking in return.

> *O Jerusalem, Jerusalem, the one who kills the prophets and stones those who are sent to her! How often I wanted to gather your children together, as a hen gathers her chicks under her wings, but you were not willing! See! Your house is left to you desolate; for I say to you, you shall see Me no more till you say, "Blessed is He who comes in the name of the Lord!"*
> — Matthew 23:37–39

This proclamation is scary to the disciples. This is the Messiah Yeshua, Who calms the waves, casts out demons, raises the dead, and more. He has just proclaimed that everything in the world is about to change. This city and, more importantly, this house that has been the center of worship for Israel and the entire world is going to be desolate? How can this be?

Jews and Gentiles in the nations who believed in the God of Israel and had the means to do so traveled to this place. Remember the Ethiopian Eunuch from the book of Acts? The God of Israel was known throughout the world, mostly for the Temple and the city of Jerusalem. How could it be that the Holy One of Israel would destroy Jerusalem and the Temple?

So he arose and went. And behold, a man of Ethiopia,
a eunuch of great authority under Candace the queen
of the Ethiopians, who had charge of all her treasury,
and had come to Jerusalem to worship…

— Acts 8:27

These Jewish disciples of Jesus did not understand and needed clarification. The questions they ask are more profound and timely than most in the world can imagine. The answers are shaking the nations of the world today like labor pains.

Then Jesus went out and departed from the temple,
and His disciples came up to show Him the buildings
of the temple.
And Jesus said to them, "Do you not see all these
things? Assuredly, I say to you, not one stone shall
be left here upon another, that shall not be thrown
down."

— Matthew 24:1–2

The disciples of the Lord are reminding Him — you know, the Creator of the world — of the importance and significance of the great Temple in Jerusalem, as if He didn't know. He then tells them prophetically what we know has taken place historically, just like our Lord Yeshua prophesied. The Romans destroyed Jerusalem and the Temple almost forty years later.

Now as He sat on the Mount of Olives, the disciples
came to Him privately, saying, "Tell us, when will

these things be? And what will be the sign of Your
coming, and of the end of the age?"
— Matthew 24:3

The disciples ask very Jewish questions according to covenant and prophecy, such as when will this take place, because they connect these events with the fulfillment of all the things that will end this age. The sign of His coming and the end of the age speak of Messiah Jesus coming to reign as King, sitting on the throne of David. This ends the times of the Gentiles ruling over Jerusalem and ushers in the Messianic Age of Day of The Lord.

Of course, we know that the Temple being destroyed was part of the plan. The Holy Spirit will dwell in born-again people who will be living stones constructing a Kingdom Temple all over the world — Hallelujah! Our Savior answers His disciples according to His prophetic plans:

> *And Jesus answered and said to them: "Take heed that*
> *no one deceives you. For many will come in My name,*
> *saying, "I am the Christ, and will deceive many. And*
> *you will hear of wars and rumors of wars. See that*
> *you are not troubled; for all these things must come to*
> *pass, but the end is not yet."*
— Matthew 24:4–6

Our Savior tells them that deception, false Christs, ongoing wars, and the threat of wars will seemingly mark the Second Coming of the Lord. He warns them that these things, in and of themselves, are not signs of the end of this age.

The next passages, however, tell us the signs the disciples in their day and we in ours should be watching for. These birth pains include human tragedies that have been taking place down through the ages.

There are three primary distinctions that make these signs unique to one generation in history. One distinction is the co-ordination of all of them coming together at the same time. The second is their coordination with two other primary biblically prophetic signs that will be addressed in some detail. The third is their frequency and intensity, which will increase until the Son of David sits on His throne.

> *For nation will rise against nation, and kingdom against kingdom. And there will be famines, pestilences, and earthquakes in various places. All these are the beginning of sorrows.*
> — Matthew 24:7–8

The New Covenant Scriptures were originally written in first-century Greek. Let's begin looking at the word "sorrows" in the passage above. The Greek word means "labor or birth pains." The English translation reflects how they would have said "birth pains" in Old English.

The word translated "nation" in this passage would be pronounced "ethnos" in English, from which you can easily hear the word ethnic. This passage speaks of a time when, like never before, ethnic groups will rise up against each other; race wars if you will. The phrase "nation against nation and kingdom against kingdom" has been understood by some scholars as an ancient Jewish saying regarding global military conflict: world war.

World Wars I and II certainly fit the bill. There has never been anything like these wars in history. Also, they were instrumental in bringing the Jews back to Israel.

From the signing of the Balfour Declaration in 1917 until Israel was declared the Jewish state, there was ongoing tension and fighting between the Jewish people and their neighbors. When we think of Israel's labor pains, the day May 14, 1948, was only the beginning of bringing the newborn to physical birth. Immediately after becoming a state once again, Israel was attacked by the armies of five nations: Egypt, Syria, Jordan, Iraq, and Lebanon. Additionally, there are reports of soldiers from Yemen and Saudi Arabia joining the labor party. Though Israel became a nation in one day, few believed it would survive more than one day. Miraculously, the tiny, seemingly doomed newborn prevailed and survived, and Israel was physically reborn.

Remember, the Isaiah 66 passage proclaims the earth will be made to give birth in a day. The two world wars shook the nations of the earth, bringing Israel to its physical birth. However, this just marks the beginning of the ethnic conflicts and wars, because the labor pains must intensify to bring Israel to its spiritual and eternal birth.

As It Goes with Israel, So It Goes with the Nations

Just before and at the beginning of World War II, few in the world could have imagined that the Nazi war machine would be able to accomplish so much in such a short period of time.

Germany was not much bigger than the state of Oregon. The world's leaders did all they could to appease Hitler and avoid war, but they failed to understand a horrifying biblical truth. What the nations do to Israel and his descendants, the Lord will often do to those nations and their descendants.

Before the war, most in the world who knew about the humiliating and atrocious persecution against the Jews cared very little about it. This is because, across Europe, for so many centuries, it was kind of a sport to persecute Jews. What these people did not realize was that this cultural norm was going to bear a heavy price. The Jews truly are the canary in the coalmine — as it goes with the Jews/Israel, so it goes with the nations.

Of course, though still denied frequently, there is and was widespread knowledge about the Holocaust while it was going on. The legal term "genocide" was initiated as a result of the Nazi atrocities against the Jews. The word pertains to the targeting of ethnic groups for destruction. Sadly, from that time onward, genocides due to ethnic strife, national struggles, and despots have flourished. The situation is comparable to dropping a rock in a pond — the ripples emanate from the center. The Holocaust and aggression against Israel are the center, and the ripples are the nations.

Though there were ongoing skirmishes between Israel and its neighbors, in 1967, the nations deepened their commitment to the labor party once again. Egypt and Syria began amassing their armies against Israel's border, again threatening them with annihilation. The Israelis struck preemptively with a stunning blow from which their bully neighbors could not recover. Jordan joined in, and all three countries were humiliated before the world. The land of Israel more than doubled in size from the Six Day War!

Speaking of the world, that is exactly who stepped in, and as usual, whenever Israel is winning, the UN brokered a cessation of fighting. This simply gave Israel's enemies time to re-arm. In 1973, Israel having become over confident and complacent, Syria and Egypt attacked the Jewish nation on its most holy day — Yom Kippur. Israel was completely surprised and caught unprepared, impossibly overwhelmed, and this time it looked like all was lost; however, once again, Israel somehow won!

There are many natural and human reasons attributed to this victory. One is the support of the USA, but there are many testimonies of miraculous manifestations of heavenly interventions, such as Syrian tank commanders refusing to advance despite massively outnumbering the Israeli tanks. Their stated reason for not advancing was that *they were prevented by angels*. Remember, this is a holy war against the Holy One of Israel and His covenant land and people.

The Pond Ripples

Today, many of the world's organizations and governments support the militant Muslim enemy states, militias, terrorists, and media outlets that are enemies of Israel. This support has ebbed and flowed through the decades since the birth of modern Israel. Certainly, most of the nations have had and do have people in authority who come against Israel. Thankfully, there have been bright spots in which nations and precious souls have been blessed for blessing Israel.

It is staggering to research and see all the mass killings, orphaned children, and ethnic displacements (refugees) associated with ethnic group rising up against ethnic group since the Holocaust and the physical rebirth of Israel. Deep investigation of wars and genocide is best saved for another book; but the carnage and brutality in ethnic cleansing and wars that have resulted in the horrible and tormenting deaths of hundreds of millions of precious souls since the World Wars and the Holocaust are tragically unique to this generation. One article I read stated the number of deaths from war and oppression during the 20th century was 203 million.[2] Here is another headline sounding the alarm to wake those slumbering through this critical hour of labor pains:

"Christian Persecution and Genocide Is Worse Now than 'Any Time in History,' Report Says."[3]

Three places I am personally acquainted with are Rwanda, Burundi, and the Democratic Republic of Congo (DRC). I have developed very close friendships and ministry partners in Rwanda and the DRC. Tragically, walking through the Genocide Memorial in Kigali, Rwanda, is similar to walking through Yad Vashem — the Holocaust Memorial in Jerusalem. The same media, government, cultural marginalization, and then dehumanization that led to the Holocaust led to the genocides in these nations.

In the Rwanda Tutsi Genocide of 1994, nearly one million men, women, and children were murdered by the Hutus in one hundred days.[4] This killing spread into Burundi and the DRC. The ethnic violence had been ongoing for decades. Specific numbers are difficult to pin down.

Reports I have read and heard are five hundred thousand in Burundi and three to five and a half million in the DRC. I am not documenting figures since the numbers vary so much depending on the reporting agency. The way many of these poor souls died and the survivors' stories after having been brutalized in such horrendous ways are things I rarely discuss in detail. Sometimes I make an exception when I talk with those who question the existence of the devil and the reality of the birth pains of Bible Prophecy.

The surge in global ethnic violence since World Wars I and II have the world's inhabitants at each other's throats today. Israel and all other nations are being positioned for the final wars of Bible Prophecy, like a baby in its mother's womb being positioned for birth. Here are just some of the ethnic and religious hotspots (religious strife is often closely associated with ethnicity) recently or in the world today:

- Israel vs. Muslim countries.
- Militant Islam vs. the world.
- Muslim vs. Muslim conflicts: Syrian civil war — approximately five hundred thousand recently killed.[5]
- Iran Shite Islam vs. Saudi Arabia Sunni Islam (this conflict is across the Middle East and spreading around the world).
- African internal political/tribal conflict: Nigeria, Central African Republic, Sudan, Somalia, Burundi, the DRC Congo.
- North Korea vs. South Korea.
- China vs. Asian countries (dispute over South China Sea).
- NATO, Ukraine vs. Russia.

- Russia vs. USA (Russia flexing muscles in the Middle East in accordance with Bible Prophecy scenarios).
- USA vs. Afghanistan, Iraq, Iran, China, North Korea.
- American internal ethnic strife between Blacks and Whites.

The birth pains of ethnic groups warring against each other and subsequent global wars will continue through prophetic Biblical wars. For this book's purposes, much will not be covered in this regard. However, for greater study, here are some important Bible chapters for those who are interested:

- Psalm 83
- Isaiah 17
- Ezekiel 38–39
- Revelation 16

Famine

Like ethnic strife and wars, hunger has existed throughout human history. However, today there are almost as many hungry people on the earth as the total global population two hundred years ago. In 1804, the world population crossed the one-billion-people threshold. Today almost that many people are victims of famine, meaning, going to bed on an empty stomach each night. The numbers soar when you factor in malnutrition and lack of clean drinking water.[6]

Pestilences

A pestilence in the Bible can be a plague, which can have an animal-borne element — a disease caused by animals commonly called pests or some unknown virus. Most people have not really faced the threat spread by diseases today. Frankly, it is frightening to consider. In my book *America's Ark*, I spend more ink on this subject, and I recommend a look at it. The deadly diseases sweeping the globe are so strange that even formerly treatable plagues now defy modern medicine such as antibiotics. Add to those the ones borne by animals, and you really get a biblical picture: AIDS (possibly animal-related), bird flu, pig flu, dengue fever, malaria, Zika virus, and many more. The most dangerous animal on the planet today is the mosquito.

And, as I update this book with a Second Edition — the entire world has faced a deadly global pandemic (pestilence) called Covid.

Additionally, warnings abound that more deadly global diseases are on the way!

Not very long ago, geography played an important part in preventing the rapid spread of pandemics because international travel was much less of an issue. But now, with the ease and low cost of global travel like never before in history comes the potential of sharing different "bugs" and diseases all over the world. When a recent Ebola outbreak in West Africa was spreading, there was great debate about allowing travelers from the hot regions into other countries. Pestilence is one of the birth pains that will intensify in this generation.

Also, at the time of this Second Edition Uganda is having an Ebola outbreak. Countries are grappling with how to screen travelers from East Africa.

Earthquakes in Various Places

He shakes the earth out of its place, And its pillars tremble...

— Job 9:6

Today the world is unifying like never before through the United Nations and other internationally coordinated organizations. There is a very clear agenda that is anti-Christ, anti-righteousness, and certainly anti-Israel. As this takes place on an unprecedented level, the LORD is shaking the earth like never before. Quite literally — the earth is shaking under the weight of its sin (Romans 8:22).

It is fitting for earth's birth pains to shake the earth. I am going to provide some statistics, but I really do not need them. Having been alive more than half a century, I see what is going on in the earth compared to how it used to be. I see and hear that the earth is shaking now in an unusual way. Think of this: many news articles have posted Oklahoma as the earthquake capital of the world![7] Strange, very strange indeed.

Earthquakes are becoming more frequent and intense, just like birth pains.[8, 9, 10] The United States Geological Survey (USGS) tells us that major earthquakes have increased 1,200% in the last 40-50 years!

"In the past 40-50 years, our records show that we have exceeded the long-term average number of major earthquakes about a dozen times." [11]

The four phenomena of ethnic violence and wars, famines, pestilences, and earthquakes have been taking place all through human history. However, when they operate in conjunction with one another, Israel's labor pains, and the other signs that are upon the world today; we can clearly see these are the four birth pains our Savior Messiah Yeshua spoke about to His disciples.

CHAPTER 7

The Fig Tree Generation

Now learn this parable from the fig tree...
— Matthew 24:32

After the birth pains passage of Matthew 24, Messiah Yeshua summarizes what will be the season of the earth's greatest tribulation. This unimaginably troubled period will end with the glorious coming of Messiah Jesus, who will sit on the throne of David! These passages lead us to the enigmatic subject of the "Fig Tree Generation."

> *For then there will be great tribulation, such as has not been since the beginning of the world until this time, no, nor ever shall be.*
> — Matthew 24:21

> *Immediately after the tribulation of those days the sun will be darkened, and the moon will not give its light; the stars will fall from heaven, and the powers of the heavens will be shaken. Then the sign of the Son of Man will appear in heaven, and then all the tribes of the earth will mourn, and they will see the Son of*

Man coming on the clouds of heaven with power and
great glory.

— Matthew 24:29–30

Then our Savior gives us another sign. Not only is it *a* sign; it is *the* primary sign. It answers the disciples' questions regarding the end of this age and the Second Coming of Messiah Jesus to reign from Jerusalem. The first distinction of this primary sign is it comes in the form of a parable or physical analogy. The allegory comes with a command to learn and understand its meaning:

> *Now learn this parable from the fig tree: When its*
> *branch has already become tender and puts forth*
> *leaves, you know that summer is near. So you also,*
> *when you see all these things, know that it is near —*
> *at the doors! Assuredly, I say to you, this generation*
> *will by no means pass away till all these things take*
> *place. Heaven and earth will pass away, but My*
> *words will by no means pass away.*
>
> *— Matthew 24:32–35*

One great mystery to me is why this parable isn't being searched out and clearly taught by every pastor or church leader in the world. Why would I say such a thing? The command by our Master, Savior, and King Yeshua is "NOW LEARN THIS PARABLE." He doesn't say, "If you have time after having done other things that are more important, then, in your spare time, please learn this parable." That being the case,

together with the appropriate urgency, let's obey Messiah Yeshua and learn this parable.

First, we need to identify the fig tree. This will be easier if we
remember why it is mentioned in the first place. Remember,
Messiah Jesus is speaking of events surrounding His return
to Jerusalem. The holy city's inhabitants would be crying out,
"Blessed is He who comes in the name of the LORD." His
disciples then ask about the sign of His coming. Since the fig
tree is the central sign, certainly it could have something to do
with Israel, right?

As we consider the fig tree Messiah speaks of in Matthew
24, can we think of a place in the Bible where Israel is called
the fig tree? Not only is there such a passage, it involves Israel
being overrun militarily. Additionally, it involves Israel being
overwhelmed at the end of this age. This lines up perfectly with
Israel and the nations' labor pains — along with other end-
times scenarios!

Awake, you drunkards, and weep; And wail, all you
drinkers of wine, Because of the new wine,
For it has been cut off from your mouth.
For a nation has come up against My land,
Strong, and without number;
His teeth are the teeth of a lion, And he has the
fangs of a fierce lion. He has laid waste My vine,
And ruined My fig tree;
He has stripped it bare and thrown it away; Its
branches are made white.

— Joel 1:5–7

> *Alas for the day!*
> *For the day of the LORD is at hand;*
> *It shall come as destruction from the Almighty.*
>   — Joel 1:15

Here, the LORD calls His Land — His fig tree! Certainly, we can see that the Covenant Land is His Land Israel. As I mentioned, we can also see the end-of-this-age component of this answer to the disciples' question in that the fig tree will be stripped bare during the Day of The Lord. The Day of The Lord involves events such as the Rapture and the Tribulation Period that lead up to the coming of Messiah Jesus to sit on the throne of David. Again, this answers the disciples' questions!

A confusing interpretation of this Joel 1 passage should be identified and addressed. Some prophecy students and teachers miss something important, only seeing the ancient Babylonian empire judging Judah. Ancient Babylon is called a lion in Daniel 7, but the final one-world empire is likened to a lion as well (Revelation 13:2). The final Gentile global empire of Daniel 7 has the combined physical characteristics of the other three strategic global empires, which are given powerful predatory animal characteristics in that same chapter: the lion, bear, and leopard. The passage from Joel 1 certainly also refers to the end-times scenario, proven by the prophetic term "Day of The Lord."

Now let's consider this: fig trees first put forth leaves, and then, in the early summer, they bear fruit. Israel "putting forth leaves," therefore, speaks of the physical birth of Israel (leaves) without the spiritual birth (fruit), as we saw in Isaiah 66. What we see from Joel is that just before the coming of Messiah

Jesus (Day of The Lord), Israel, like a fig tree, will be stripped bare. How could that be the case if Israel were not yet physically reborn? We are living now in the Fig Tree Generation!

Messiah Yeshua told us the generation that sees the fig tree put forth leaves will not pass away before "*all these things take place*" that are spoken of in Matthew 24. This is so incredible and difficult to imagine — His Second Coming to reign as King will take place in the generation that witnesses Israel once again becoming a nation! Stop for just a moment and let that sink in.

Next, the obvious questions are: how long is a generation, and when does the countdown begin? The word "generation" is used in different ways and in different contexts. Why should that matter regarding our generation question? There is a fundamental Bible interpretation principle that can prevent us from misunderstanding the word of God. Here it is: CONTEXT IS KING!

If you were to ask me to define the word "run," I would ask you for some context. Are you asking me about my nose when I have the flu, my refrigerator, or my morning jog? So it should be when we think about the word "generation" when speaking of the prophetic fig tree.

Is there anywhere in the Bible where the word "generation" is used to explain a scenario where the Jews have been driven out of the Promised Land, and then, according to the covenant promise, told they would return? The answer is YES! I have read the entire Bible many times, and there is only one place I know of that fits the bill. Here is the kicker — this is the passage where the LORD is cutting the covenant with Abram (later named Abraham), sealing the Abraham Covenant!

Now when the sun was going down, a deep sleep fell
upon Abram; and behold, horror and great dark-
ness fell upon him. Then He said to Abram: "Know
certainly that your descendants will be strangers in
a land that is not theirs, and will serve them, and
they will afflict them four hundred years. And also
the nation whom they serve I will judge; afterward
they shall come out with great possessions. Now as for
you, you shall go to your fathers in peace; you shall be
buried at a good old age. But in the fourth generation
they shall return here, for the iniquity of the Amorites
is not yet complete.

— Genesis 15:12–16

Here, we find the Jewish people would be driven out of the Promised Land, endure great affliction, and then return to what would later be called Israel. Father Abraham was promised this absence would last four hundred years, and then, in the fourth generation, the children of Israel would return. If four hundred years is four generations, then how many years is one generation? It is one hundred years — and the context fits perfectly! The LORD proved He meant what He said. Elohim delivered the children of Israel out of Egypt in four generations. Messiah Yeshua will certainly do so and return to Israel in one generation — the "Fig Tree Generation"!

I have heard many explanations and listened to intricate calculations used to define a generation, but they just do not fit like this. Rarely do they have anything to do with the covenants to interpret the prophecies. Yet if we simply look at the promises and trust Adonai to keep them perfectly, it all becomes much simpler to understand. We can also find anchors within the covenants to help us understand the prophecies — like the word "generation."

Here is something else to consider. The book of Hebrews has a famous chapter, often called "the hall of faith." Of course, this is chapter 11, and interestingly, Father Abraham gets the most press in this special club of faith. Actually, we see Abraham used as a great example throughout the entire Bible regarding understanding righteousness, faith, and how to know and walk with our Creator Elohim. It should be no surprise that we find the definition of the final generation of this age in the passage where the LORD cuts the covenant with Abraham.

Isaiah also instructs children of Abraham to look to him for understanding.

> *Listen to Me, you who follow after righteousness, You who seek the LORD:*
>> *Look to the rock from which you were hewn,*
>> *And to the hole of the pit from which you were dug. Look to Abraham your father, And to Sarah who bore you; For I called him alone,*
>> *And blessed him and increased him.*
> — Isaiah 51:1–2

We have seen the Bible interpret itself regarding the fig tree and the generation when our Savior will come to fulfill His covenants. The next question is: When did the fig tree become tender and put forth leaves? To answer this question, it is important to understand some little-known history of the Promised Land. When and how did the Land stop being called by its biblical name, and when was it called Israel again? You will not see this on the evening news, because it dispels so much disinformation today.

The Romans destroyed Jerusalem, and just as Messiah prophesied, they leveled the holy Temple in 70 AD. Later, in 133–135 AD, there was a final revolt against Rome by the Jewish people in Judea and Northern Israel. Most of the Jews who were not slaughtered in this uprising were taken into slavery and dispersed throughout the Roman Empire. Emperor Hadrian then gave Jerusalem the title Aelia Capitolina. The Roman leader also renamed Israel after its archenemy, the Philistines — Philistina. In English, we call it — Palestine.

For almost two thousand years, the Promised Land was known by something other than what the Word of God calls it. Yet even with this heathen name, the land continuously maintained a Jewish presence. Then, in one day, just as prophesied in the Bible, the Israeli flag went up the pole, and Israel became a nation once again. Some would debate and assert other possibilities, but I cannot think of another day that would initiate the generation clock ticking as much as that one — what a mountaintop of prophetic fulfillment!

If that is the case — and I will not be dogmatic, but it certainly appears that it is — then this has earthshaking and incredible implications for everyone on the planet today! There have been strange prophecies of specific dates set for the end of this age and, tragically, even books written that predicted dates and timetables that have come and gone. This can really wreck the faith of precious souls and, in the eyes of some, bring shame to the name of our Lord.

In Matthew 24, we are also told by our Messiah Yeshua that nobody knows the hour or day of His Second Coming to end this age. However, we are also told by the Apostle Paul that we are to know the season of the Day of The Lord. Paul also warns the Thessalonians, and we who follow Messiah today, that failing to perceive the signs of the Day of The Lord is an expression of stumbling in darkness. Interestingly, Paul also speaks of labor pains:

> *But of that day and hour no one knows, not even the angels of heaven, but My Father only.*
> — Matthew 24:36

> *But concerning the times and the seasons, brethren, you have no need that I should write to you. For you yourselves know perfectly that the day of the Lord so comes as a thief in the night. For when they say, "Peace and safety!" then sudden destruction comes upon them, as labor pains upon a pregnant woman. And they shall not escape. But you, brethren, are not in darkness, so that this Day should overtake you as a thief. You are all sons of light and sons of the day. We are not of the night nor of darkness.*
> — 1 Thessalonians 5:1–5

So, let's sum up the concept of the "Fig Tree Generation." The fig tree is Israel, and according to the prophecy of Isaiah 66, in one day, the Promised Land regained the name Israel after approximately nineteen hundred years! I assert that this means Israel, on May 14, 1948, began to put forth leaves. There must be yet a spiritual birth for Israel — Israel must be born from above or born again!

First, before identifying what this one-hundred-year generation means to us today, remember these words from Messiah Jesus: *"Now learn this parable from the fig tree"* (Matthew 24:32). If our Savior commands us to learn this parable and tells us all these details, including the generation that will not pass away, isn't it my obligation as His disciple to search Scripture to learn this parable? Not only is this command for first-century disciples, but for all disciples of Messiah Yeshua. This is especially true for the disciples living in the "Fig Tree Generation."

We should do our best to avoid setting dates unless Scripture demands we do so. Our Savior uses a word in this parable, one He has commanded me to learn, and that word is a measurement of time. If I am to learn this parable, then I must learn this measurement of time as well. However, it is important to be balanced. I have been careful to say that I have made assertions regarding when the one hundred years begin based on Scripture, and I believe them to be true.

Messiah Yeshua said the generation which sees the fig tree put forth leaves, along with the other signs He spoke of in Matthew 24 (which are also seen in Mark 13 and Luke 21), will not pass away until Messiah returns to the earth. We have seen from Father Abraham that a generation in this context is one hundred years. If these things I am asserting are accurate interpretations of God's word — and obviously, I believe they are — then we are living in the last generation of this age. We are living in the final generation, which will witness King Messiah Yeshua sitting on His throne! I am not setting a date, an hour, or a day; I am identifying the season.

I have been told by some that we cannot know what the fig tree is or exactly what a generation means. So, let me get this straight — the Lord commanded me to learn something I cannot learn — is that it? The truth is, so many different opinions of this passage have been wrong because they have not properly defined the fig tree or a generation. In some cases, their opinions of the fig tree and their understanding of calculating the length of a generation have not been founded on the simple and strong foundations of covenant as it relates to prophecy.

By the grace of our Heavenly Abba Father, through Messiah Yeshua, and by the revelation from the Holy Spirit, we CAN learn this parable! Also, through the good old-fashioned work of studying Scripture and learning from other faithful teachers over the years, in some measure, I have learned this passage according to the commands of my Savior.

Having done so and having shared it with you the reader, there is one more primary sign to look at before sharing the best part of Matthew 24. After this sign, we will see the way to live for anyone on earth who truly loves our Adonai Yeshua. The way has been prepared to facilitate fruitful and successful living in this "Fig Tree Generation" — the last generation of this age!

CHAPTER 8

The Days of Noah and the Last of the Last Days

The LORD sat enthroned at the Flood, And the
LORD sits as King forever.

— Psalm 29:10

The next major sign after the fig tree clearly demonstrates to the earth's inhabitants that they live in the final generation of this age. This one operates in perfect synergy with the physical rebirth of Israel and the birth pains of the nations. It is the sign of the "Days of Noah." Oh, that people today would hear these words and quickly make adjustments!

> *But of that day and hour no one knows, not even the*
> *angels of heaven, but My Father only. But as the days*
> *of Noah were, so also will the coming of the Son of*
> *Man be. For as in the days before the flood, they were*
> *eating and drinking, marrying and giving in mar-*
> *riage, until the day that Noah entered the ark, and*
> *did not know until the flood came and took them all*
> *away, so also will the coming of the Son of Man be.*
> — Matthew 24:36–39

The first verse (*"But of that day and hour..."*) has deeper meaning than first meets the eye and will be addressed in the next chapter. However, once again, we clearly see that, though we cannot know the hour or day, we can know the season of the coming of Messiah Yeshua. He gives us a very important comparison that would be hard to miss for someone who is really watching.

Messiah tells us that the way it was in Noah's generation will be very similar to the season of the coming of the Lord. Adonai Yeshua warns that in the generation of His coming, people will be living like they were in Noah's day and, similarly, will be going on with their lives as usual. Yet the wrath of God will bear down on this final generation, and great destruction will consume them.

Having said that, if we look back to Noah's time, what will we find? There are primary characteristics in Genesis 6 that will help us understand the "Days of Noah" so we can compare his day to ours. Having taught this many times, I am still amazed at the likeness of the two generations despite being so far apart in time.

> *Now it came to pass, when men began to multiply on the face of the earth, and daughters were born to them, that the sons of God saw the daughters of men, that they were beautiful; and they took wives for themselves of all whom they chose.*
>
> — Genesis 6:1–2

The first thing we see in Noah's generation is a population explosion: *"men began to multiply on the earth."* One thing that is often forgotten is that sin continuously spreads on the earth, bringing with it great death and destruction. How has sin spread on the earth? The Bible clearly answers that question.

> *Therefore, just as through one man sin entered the world, and death through sin, and thus death spread to all men, because all sinned...*
> — Romans 5:12

It is the sin of mankind, beginning with Adam, that has not only killed the people on earth, it also makes the earth travail. This travailing is like a woman in labor and has intensified into the "end-of-this-age birth pains" that have been discussed thus far.

Paul the apostle wrote about this as well. He was looking forward to the time when those who have been raptured will return with Messiah Jesus in resurrected bodies that are without sin. This is also called *the revealing of the sons of God.*

> *For the earnest expectation of the creation eagerly waits for the revealing of the sons of God. For the creation was subjected to futility, not willingly, but because of Him who subjected it in hope; because the creation itself also will be delivered from the bondage of corruption into the glorious liberty of the children of God. For we know that the whole creation groans and labors with birth pangs together until now.*
> — Romans 8:19–22

Since we see creation shaking under the weight of sin on earth, we can see why a population explosion like in Noah's day would make the earth travail in birth pains all the more. Could it be that the birth pains of Israel and the nations discussed thus far are also linked to a population explosion of sinners? That is exactly what is happening.

In the year 1804, there were 1,000,000,000 (one billion) people on planet earth. Today, just a little over two hundred years later, earth's population is 8,000,000,000 — eight billion people. I think we can all agree — that is a population explosion! Remember, Paul spoke of the bondage of corruption from which the earth would be delivered. Seven billion more people living on earth in sin-corrupted bodies would understandably make the earth travail like never before!

> *And the LORD said, "My Spirit shall not strive with man forever, for he is indeed flesh; yet his days shall be one hundred and twenty years."*
>
> — Genesis 6:3

> *Then the LORD saw that the wickedness of man was great in the earth, and that every intent of the thoughts of his heart was only evil continually. And the LORD was sorry that He had made man on the earth, and He was grieved in His heart. So the LORD said, "I will destroy man whom I have created from the face of the earth, both man and beast, creeping thing and birds of the air, for I am sorry that I have made them."*
>
> — Genesis 6:5–7

Adonai set the span of one hundred twenty years before wiping out almost the entire earth's population. It may be good to think about that concept and compare it to your belief in God. How could a loving God do such a thing? It is because this loving Elohim, the true and living God, is holy and righteous as much as He is love! The holiness and righteousness of Elohim was so greatly offended that His righteous wrath had to be executed.

There is another reason for the flood that should be mentioned. Back in the third chapter of Genesis, Elohim promised that a man-child would come from Eve, who would destroy the works of the devil. Satan, who had hijacked a serpent's body, deceived Eve, while Adam knowingly disobeyed the LORD. They committed the first sin of mankind. After pronouncing specific curses on Adam and Eve, Adonai Elohim then turns to Satan.

> *So the LORD God said to the serpent:*
> *"Because you have done this, You are cursed more than all cattle, And more than every beast of the field; On your belly you shall go, And you shall eat dust All the days of your life. And I will put enmity Between you and the woman, And between your seed and her Seed; He shall bruise your head, And you shall bruise His heel."*
> — Genesis 3:14–15

With that understood, it is easier to see Satan's strategy. The diabolical plan was to corrupt mankind to such a degree it would be impossible to bring a righteous man into the earth who would destroy the wicked one. The only problem with the plan is that it schemes against the One who never loses and who always has a better plan!

Wickedness was so great on the earth that it became a place of great corruption. Corruption refers to something decayed, ruined, and rotten.

There is an analogy a pastor gave that I never forgot. He was from Louisiana, in the USA, and lived in an area prone to hurricanes. A really severe one ripped through his town, wreaking much havoc and devastation. Having personally experienced Hurricane Ike in Houston, Texas, and having witnessed, along with the rest of the world, the record-breaking Hurricane Harvey in Houston, it is easy to understand the next step — cleanup duty.

Louisiana is a place that gets very hot and humid. Many days after the hurricane, they found a meat freezer that was tossed in an open field and had been sitting in the sun for many blistering, sunny days. The pastor told of the stench and decay of the meat that the senses experienced after opening the freezer lid. "Eeeeww" is the word that comes to mind. That is corruption. The meat was so rotten and disgusting the only thing to do with it was to destroy it — fast!

> *The earth also was corrupt before God, and the earth was filled with violence. So God looked upon the earth, and indeed it was corrupt; for all flesh had corrupted their way on the earth.*
> — Genesis 6:11–12

And God said to Noah, "The end of all flesh has come before Me, for the earth is filled with violence through them; and behold, I will destroy them with the earth.
— Genesis 6:13

Extreme violence was also a characteristic of Noah's time, as it is mentioned twice along with corruption. Society had become so rotten and violent that almost everyone was beyond redemption and would be destroyed. This is the darkness of Noah's time.

There we have it — the primary reasons for the flood of Noah are clearly proclaimed in Genesis 6 in the bestselling book of all time — the Bible. They are: a multiplying of people (population explosion), unchecked wickedness leading to widespread corruption, and global violence.

We have already identified the population explosion in our generation, but what about the other characteristics: violence, wickedness, and corruption? Certainly, today they are worse than ever!

Violence

We could note many strange and tragic statistics regarding violence today, and some have already been established. But here is an important question: When and where should be the safest time and place in any human being's life? It is when a person is a baby in their mother's womb. Yet today, it is the most dangerous time and place.

We need to remember something parenthetically unique to this generation before I give a statistic. For all who would seek it, there is forgiveness, healing, and love in Messiah Yeshua.

His love can wash away every sin and make the vilest sinner clean — even me!

There are over 40,000,000 (forty million) babies killed in their mother's womb every year. If you add up the number of babies murdered every year going back to 1980 and then compare it to deaths caused by war and genocide, it is shocking. The number of dead babies would double the number of deaths caused by war and genocide over the last two thousand years — COMBINED! The actual number of babies murdered by abortion going back to 1980 is approximately 1,500,000,000 (one and a half billion!).[12] The abortion clock ticks so quickly that it is heartbreaking to imagine how many more babies will have died by the time you read this.

The violent culture of abortion is not limited to women who carry the babies and men who father them. Supreme Court justices, politicians and their constituents, doctors, nurses, administrative staff of abortion centers, and everyone else who in any way facilitates and promotes abortion all make up this mere snapshot of the violent culture of this unique modern "Days of Noah."

Wickedness: The Wrath of Elohim Revealed from Heaven!

On one occasion, I was listening to Barack Obama while campaigning for president in 2008. He was actually preaching the Bible and telling people that our Lord Jesus legitimized homosexuality in the Sermon on the Mount.[13] Mr. Obama went on to explain that since this was the case, he was unconcerned regarding an obscure passage in the book of Romans. Well, let me share with you that obscure passage, along with the other verses preceding and following to confirm the context:

> *For the wrath of God is revealed from heaven against all ungodliness and unrighteousness of men, who suppress the truth in unrighteousness, because what may be known of God is manifest in them, for God has shown it to them. For since the creation of the world His invisible attributes are clearly seen, being understood by the things that are made, even His eternal power and Godhead, so that they are without excuse, because, although they knew God, they did not glorify Him as God, nor were thankful, but became futile in their thoughts, and their foolish hearts were darkened.*
> — Romans 1:18–21

There are certain things that provoke the wrath of our Heavenly Abba Father. Knowingly suppressing the truth in unrighteousness so as to rob Elohim of His glory is so very offensive to Him. Additionally, we live because of Him — breathe His air, kill and eat His animals, use His creation for so many purposes, etc. In addition, His only begotten Son died for us so that we could have eternal life. After all of this grace and mercy, if widespread unthankfulness permeates global society — wrath is on the way!

Futility and darkness blanket the minds and hearts of people in this kind of culture just like in the days of Noah. Let's take a look at the characteristics of such a society. Then we can compare them to ours today.

Professing to be wise, they became fools, and changed the glory of the incorruptible God into an image made like corruptible man — and birds and four-footed animals and creeping things.

— Romans 1:22–23

In the great foolishness of this generation, people profess to be wise while promoting the widely accepted dark theory that people are like God. Mankind is the sum total of the equation of natural selection. Not created, but the strongest and fittest of our ancestors — birds, four-footed animals, and creeping things — man is the pinnacle of evolution. Mankind is the grandmaster of the universe — not!

As a result of such widespread foolishness across the globe, the wrath of Elohim is being demonstrated by fulfilling His word. He has turned so much of the world over to its wicked devices that corruption is rampant. This blind inability to resist wickedness is not only going to bring the wrath of God — it is the wrath of God! This wrath is revealed from heaven against all ungodliness and unrighteousness of men!

It is very similar to the judgment upon Israel when they were immersed in sin and worshipped the false gods of the Assyrians and Babylonians. Elohim demonstrated that if Israel did not want the LORD but wanted these other gods, which were actually demon spirits, then the Jewish people could have these foreign deities. In addition, Israel got all that came with the worship of false gods — great destruction and death. Today, Elohim is simply letting people have what they want and all that comes with it.

Therefore God also gave them up to uncleanness, in the lusts of their hearts, to dishonor their bodies among themselves, who exchanged the truth of God for the lie, and worshiped and served the creature rather than the Creator, who is blessed forever. Amen.

— Romans 1:24–25

The only way to live in this kind of flagrant sin and still sleep at night is to exchange the truth of Elohim for the lie. What is the lie? It is the false assertion that we (created people) do not need to worship and serve our Creator. Instead, we embrace the worship of creation, which fits very nicely with evolution and false religions.

I already touched on evolution, but why false religions? The lie of false religions accomplishes two things: it helps one to maintain control of their own life (be their own god) while still enjoying the false notion of a nice afterlife. False religions tell the lie: "Be a good person and believe in whatever god, and this is enough for a nice life after death." So then, dead religion and evolution (which is very popular with atheists and humanists) facilitate the lie — man is at the center of everything, not Elohim the Father, Son, and Holy Spirit.

This uniquely offensive rejection of our Creator provokes a response from Him that facilitates the kind of society we see in Noah's time. The rottenness is so ingrained into the fabric of the culture of the people that the LORD gives them over to their lust, which is an expression of His wrath! Lust is a strong desire for that which Elohim forbids. The number one sin in a long list that clearly identifies such a society is the acceptance, legitimization, and promotion of homosexuality.

For this reason God gave them up to vile passions. For even their women exchanged the natural use for what is against nature. Likewise also the men, leaving the natural use of the woman, burned in their lust for one another, men with men committing what is shameful, and receiving in themselves the penalty of their error which was due.

— Romans 1:26–27

Immoral Morality

The most glaring expression of the corruption today that so mirrors Noah's time, as well as that of Sodom and Gomorrah, is the aptly called "fascist homosexual movement." I will address why it is called "fascist" in a moment. But first, let's consider how it has permeated the culture.

Like never before, homosexual relationships are presented as legitimate in much of the world today. Through media, legislation, educational systems, the military, and even false churches, homosexuality is revered, protected, and celebrated. Actually, in this sick generation, there is a stigma attached to believing same-sex marriage and relationships are wrong.

The homosexual political machine is akin to fascism because of the forcible suppression of opposition that it wields. For example, there are bakers, florists, and bed and breakfast owners who are losing everything, including their businesses and other financial resources, due to sky-high fines that are almost impossible to pay. Discrimination laws have been passed in an effort to force everyone to participate in this madness!

Imagine, perverted sexual behavior has been elevated to the sacred level of something so beautiful as ethnicity. What a strange time. If someone objects in any public way to this horrible perversion, then they are considered a bigot!

Today, it is not surprising to attempt to watch a sporting event on television, only to be verbally assaulted by a sports journalist who is not speaking about sports. Instead, he is preaching the virtues of same-sex marriage. And though all a poor soul wanted to know was the score of the ballgame, he is called immoral for not agreeing with homosexual marriage. It is immoral morality. The Prophet Isaiah uses the strongest word of warning: "woe."

> *Woe to those who call evil good, and good evil; Who put darkness for light, and light for darkness; Who put bitter for sweet, and sweet for bitter!*
>
> — Isaiah 5:20

It has been said by preachers that widespread government-sanctioned homosexuality brings the wrath of God. But after a closer look at the first chapter of Romans, it would be more accurate to say that this kind of "Noah's day" corruption "IS" the wrath of God. The physical execution of it must then be right around the corner.

In Romans 1, there is a long list of other sins that accompany widespread homosexuality. They too are important as they also make up the fabric of a society under the wrath of the LORD. These other offenses make up a tapestry of wickedness, corruption, and violence. Yet this tapestry of sins is explained and categorized very specifically in Paul's second letter to his disciple Timothy. Let's compare Romans 1 to 2 Timothy 3:

And even as they did not like to retain God in their knowledge, God gave them over to a debased mind, to do those things which are not fitting; being filled with all unrighteousness, sexual immorality, wickedness, covetousness, maliciousness; full of envy, murder, strife, deceit, evil-mindedness; they are whisperers, backbiters, haters of God, violent, proud, boasters, inventors of evil things, disobedient to parents, undiscerning, untrustworthy, unloving, unforgiving, unmerciful; who, knowing the righteous judgment of God, that those who practice such things are deserving of death, not only do the same but also approve of those who practice them.

— Romans 1:28–32

But know this, that in the last days perilous times will come: For men will be lovers of themselves, lovers of money, boasters, proud, blasphemers, disobedient to parents, unthankful, unholy, unloving, unforgiving, slanderers, without self-control, brutal, despisers of good, traitors, headstrong, haughty, lovers of pleasure rather than lovers of God, having a form of godliness but denying its power. And from such people turn away!

— 2 Timothy 3:1–5

Since Paul tells Timothy that these times will come in the last days, there is an important question to ask: when did the last days begin? We find the answer in the second chapter of the book of Acts.

The Holy Spirit has just fallen upon the disciples of Yeshua during Shavuot (Pentecost). Messiah has already ascended to heaven after His glorious resurrection, and He promised this day would come — the birth of the New Covenant Ecclesia (Church)! The disciples are speaking to a crowd in Jerusalem gathered from many nations and languages. There are signs and wonders taking place — these Galileans are even preaching in the languages of those from the nations. Some are scoffing and accusing the preachers of drunkenness.

> But Peter, standing up with the eleven, raised his voice and said to them, "Men of Judea and all who dwell in Jerusalem,
>
> let this be known to you, and heed my words. For these are not drunk, as you suppose, since it is only the third hour of the day. But this is what was spoken by the prophet Joel: 'And it shall come to pass in the last days, says God,
>
> That I will pour out of My Spirit on all flesh; Your sons and your daughters shall prophesy, Your young men shall see visions,
>
> Your old men shall dream dreams.
>
> And on My menservants and on My maidservants I will pour out My Spirit in those days;
>
> And they shall prophesy.

I will show wonders in heaven above And signs in the earth beneath:

Blood and fire and vapor of smoke. The sun shall be turned into darkness, And the moon into blood,

Before the coming of the great and awesome day of the Lord. And it shall come to pass

That whoever calls on the name of the Lord Shall be saved.'

— Acts 2:14–21

We see and hear Peter preaching from the Prophet Joel that the last days began on that day in Jerusalem. Some of what Joel wrote is yet to be fulfilled (though it will be very soon), but much has already been fulfilled. So, there you have it — the last days began in the first century.

If that is true, what is Paul saying when he writes "in the last days perilous times will come"? The answer is that he is writing about a specific generation, the last generation, just before the coming of Messiah Yeshua! Paul is not only talking about the last days — he is defining the last of the last days.

What does this have to do with Noah? "The Days of Noah," the Romans 1 generation, and the last of the last days are all the same. Instead of a flood, look at what is coming. By His word, the LORD judged the earth with water in Noah's time. By the same word of Elohim, He is about to judge the earth with fire.

For this they willfully forget: that by the word of God the heavens were of old, and the earth standing out of water and in the water, by which the world that

then existed perished, being flooded with water. But
the heavens and the earth which are now preserved
by the same word, are reserved for fire until the day of
judgment and perdition of ungodly men.

— 2 Peter 3:5–7

Is there any good news? Yes, and the good news is so extremely good that it provides great hope and confidence even in view of the great wrath which is coming! Noah found something that is available today. The next chapter should cheer us up tremendously.

CHAPTER 9

Noah's Day,
the Jewish Wedding,
and the Rapture

But of that day and hour...
— Matthew 24:36

This earthshaking end-times sign (the Days of Noah) is introduced with a Jewish cultural saying, or "Hebraism." It is essential to understand the saying as it relates to this end of the age sign. Messiah Yeshua uses the term from an ancient Jewish ceremony. First, let's read the verse again:

> *But of that day and hour no one knows, not even the angels of heaven, but My Father only.*
> — Matthew 24:36

Once again, I am touching on something that could fill the pages of an entire book. The Jewish wedding traditions during the time of Messiah at His first coming were quite prophetic. Actually, Messiah partially fulfilled these ceremonies and rituals and will finish doing so through Bible Prophecy.

The scenario begins with the father selecting a bride for his son. Long before a wedding ceremony, the father and his son would go to the home of the future bride. The groom's father and his son would propose a dowry to be paid. A marriage contract called a "ketubah," would have been written and agreed upon. The agreement included the "bride price." Sounds kind of like a covenant — yes? Our Father in heaven so loved the world that He sent His only begotten Son to pay the New Covenant "bride price."

Messiah Yeshua paid for our sins, bought us with His precious blood, and then He rose from the grave! The words "it is finished," meaning "paid in full," continue to beckon us to what is called the "Marriage Supper of the Lamb." Soon, through the upcoming chapters, we will see this match made in heaven unfold through the Prophetic Scriptures.

After the wedding agreement, the groom would go back to his father's house and begin the task of building a suitable place for his bride. This was known as the time of "betrothal." How would the groom know when the task was completed? The job was finished only when his father inspected and gave his approval. Only the father knew the "day and the hour" when the work was completed, at which time the son was released to go and get his bride.

Messiah Jesus said that He was going to our Father's house to prepare a place for us — the bride of Messiah (John 14:2–3). He also promised to take us back to that place He has been preparing for almost two thousand years! The groom would most often come late in the evening, unannounced, and at no certain time.

The bride, who had no idea when the groom would return, was to prepare herself to be his wife and be ready for him to come for her. Since the betrothed's life was consumed with great expectation of the groom coming at any moment to take her away, she lived with great hope that "today might be the day!"

When will the Messiah Groom-Yeshua come for His bride? In fulfillment of the Jewish wedding and the word of God, "nobody knows the day and the hour" but our Heavenly Abba Father. Let's continue to look at the Days of Noah passage in the light of unfolding prophetic New Covenant passages. We can then determine with certainty what Messiah Yeshua is saying to His betrothed in Matthew 24:36.

Some, at first glance, may think that Adonai is talking exclusively about His Second Coming to reign and rule on earth when He speaks of "that day and hour." Yet, later in the unfolding New Covenant Scriptures, there is a mysterious event that is demystified and clearly explained. This incredible occurrence is commonly known as "the Rapture."

You may remember at this book's first mention of the Second Coming of Messiah that a brief distinction was made regarding the event called the "Rapture," or "Catching Away," of born-again believers. Now is an important time to address this a bit more. We can begin to unpack what the Apostle Paul called a mystery that was being revealed. Much more will be shared about the Rapture, but for the sake of understanding the "Days of Noah," it is essential to share more now as it relates to "But of that day and hour…"

Introductory Rapture Passages:

Now this I say, brethren, that flesh and blood cannot inherit the kingdom of God; nor does corruption inherit incorruption. Behold, I tell you a mystery: We shall not all sleep, but we shall all be changed — in a moment, in the twinkling of an eye, at the last trumpet. For the trumpet will sound, and the dead will be raised incorruptible, and we shall be changed.

— 1 Corinthians 15:50–52

For this we say to you by the word of the Lord, that we who are alive and remain until the coming of the Lord will by no means precede those who are asleep. For the Lord Himself will descend from heaven with a shout, with the voice of an archangel, and with the trumpet of God. And the dead in Christ will rise first. Then we who are alive and remain shall be caught up together with them in the clouds to meet the Lord in the air. And thus we shall always be with the Lord.

— 1 Thessalonians 4:15–17

Paul speaks and writes about this glorious event after the time of the earthly ministry of our Adonai Yeshua. It will be glorious because, on that day, all those in Messiah will be given resurrected, glorified, sinless, eternal bodies! It is important to understand how this catching away (being caught up) relates to the Lord's teaching about Noah's day.

This mystery was not yet revealed while the Lord was on earth teaching Bible Prophecy. When Adonai says to His disciples, "of that day and hour," their only reference was His Second Coming to rule and reign from Jerusalem. Yet, since the Lord's prophetic plans unfolded further in the time of the twelve apostle's ministries, we can now apply that further revelation to Messiah's teaching in Matthew 24.

Paul taught that the mysterious resurrection, and home-going of those in Messiah, is an unannounced event that could take place any time. Paul is beginning to sound like our Adonai and Savior Yeshua. Why? Paul is also warning that no man knows the day or the hour (*in a moment*), like those in the Days of Noah and the bride of the Jewish wedding. The bride will meet the Groom in the air and go to the place He has prepared for us! Again, we should be reminded why this Rapture teaching is so important.

This homegoing takes place before the Second Coming of Messiah to sit on the throne of David. Since it has not yet taken place and these Second Coming signs are all around us, we should be looking for the Rapture even more intentionally! Messiah Yeshua coming for us in the clouds any moment is the hope He has placed within each believer. Like the bride in the Jewish wedding who is making herself ready for the groom, we should be preparing for our Messiah Groom to come! Another Apostle — John put it this way:

> *And everyone who has this hope in Him purifies himself, just as He is pure.*
>
> — 1 John 3:3

If you have been taught and believe very differently about the Rapture, please stay with me. In the upcoming "Faithful Servant" chapter, we will attempt to find a way to avoid the not-so-uncommon "Rapture hassle," as I like to call it. This is good and comforting news — not something that should bring division.

Then we who are alive and remain shall be caught up together with them in the clouds to meet the Lord in the air. And thus we shall always be with the Lord. Therefore comfort one another with these words.

— 1 Thessalonians 4:17–18

Noah's Redeemed Life and the Rapture

Nobody knows the day or hour of the coming of Messiah Jesus for His people. Also, nobody knows the day or hour Adonai Yeshua will return to sit on the Throne of David in Jerusalem. Now, let's look closer at Noah's redemption, as it provides interesting insight into the coming of Messiah in the clouds for His bride.

The Lord reminds us that what took place in Noah's day is not a fable to be dismissed. No, it was an actual event from which the wise will learn wisdom. The people lived as if the sins of Noah's day would be overlooked by Elohim, and then all but Noah's family were destroyed.

Though the time of Noah was filled with great human tragedy, if we look back at this God-touched man, we can find hope today. It is a hope that too many disciples of Messiah Jesus never consider. You see, Noah found something that made a way for him to escape the wrath of Elohim upon the earth. The Bible teaches that Noah found the LORD's grace. This same grace is also found in the Rapture.

So the LORD said, "I will destroy man whom I have created from the face of the earth, both man and beast, creeping thing and birds of the air, for I am sorry that

I have made them." But Noah found grace in the eyes
of the LORD.

— Genesis 6:7–8

First, what is grace, and what does it do? The most common definition of Elohim's uncommon grace is that it is God's goodness, which nobody deserves. Yet, it is freely given because the price for it was purchased by the blood of the Lamb Yeshua. What does grace do? We are saved by grace through faith — right?

For by grace you have been saved through faith, and
that not of yourselves; it is the gift of God, not of
works, lest anyone should boast.

— Ephesians 2:8–9

From what are we saved? We are saved from the wrath of Elohim. We are not only saved by God — we are also saved from God! Since He is just, the LORD will administer justice on the earth. His wrath is an expression of His justice. Paul explains the matter as he also writes about God's wrath as it relates to the innocent shed blood of the Lamb Yeshua:

Much more then, having now been justified by His
blood, we shall be saved from wrath through Him.

— Romans 5:9

Here is another question: what does grace do after we are saved? I will never forget this definition as long as I live: "Grace is the work of God the Father in man the sinner to change him (man the sinner) into the image of His (God the Father's) Dear Son (Messiah Yeshua)."

Here is the best passage I have found that tells us what grace actually does:

> *For the grace of God that brings salvation has appeared to all men, teaching us that, denying ungodliness and worldly lusts, we should live soberly, righteously, and godly in the present age, looking for the blessed hope and glorious appearing of our great God and Savior Jesus Christ, who gave Himself for us, that He might redeem us from every lawless deed and purify for Himself His own special people, zealous for good works.*
>
> — Titus 2:11–14

In this passage, we hear that Abba Father saves by grace yet also teaches His children by grace. If we will truly walk with Messiah Jesus, Abba's grace will constantly teach us. And look at what His grace teaches every true disciple of the Lord: to deny ungodliness and worldly lusts and also to live soberly, righteously, and godly in this present age. That means those who are saved can actually choose to do something that the unsaved cannot.

Yeshua people can actually listen to grace as it teaches them to not sin! Grace teaches us, but we can choose to listen to the Teacher or not. Sadly, so many believers choose to walk after the flesh instead of the Spirit of grace.

Many profess Messiah Jesus but do not possess Him. Since they have not been saved by grace, they certainly cannot be taught by it. Those who are instructed by grace reject ungodliness and embrace the things of Adonai Yeshua.

We also see in the Titus passage above that grace teaches us there is an end to this age. This is the "age of grace" — meaning a unique time in which there is great kindness extended by Elohim to the earth before a designated time of justice and wrath. Grace teaches born-again followers of Messiah Yeshua how to experience this great kindness of Abba Father through Messiah Yeshua and by the Ruach Ha Kodesh (Holy Spirit).

Noah found grace in that he trusted and believed in Elohim to save him and his entire house. All those in the Old Testament looked forward to the LORD saving them. They did this by grace through faith. This grace through faith operated according to the revelation given at that time. It is said this way: "We (New Testament saints) look back to the cross of Messiah Yeshua, while they (Old Testament saints) looked forward to the cross." How do we know Noah trusted and obeyed the LORD as a man saved by grace?

> *By faith Noah, being divinely warned of things not yet seen, moved with godly fear, prepared an ark for the saving of his household, by which he condemned the world and became heir of the righteousness which is according to faith.*
>
> — Hebrews 11:7

Noah's age was coming to an end. An event like never before was about to change the entire earth. Then, as the wrath of the LORD was literally being poured out, the righteous on the earth were taken away and protected from that wrath. After the wrath subsided, Noah and his family, who were redeemed by the coming Savior Messiah Yeshua, then inherited the earth!

So it will be when this age of grace ends and the tribulation begins. The wrath of the Lamb will be poured out upon the earth. Yet, those born again in Messiah Yeshua, having been redeemed by the blood of the Lamb, will be caught up in the clouds and saved from the wrath to come! The redeemed during this age will then return with Messiah Yeshua to inherit the earth.

If we look at this passage again, we can imagine the life of Noah, who, for one hundred and twenty years, lived his life's mission of building that boat. He lived a life of grace, denying the wickedness of his generation and looking for the way the LORD would save him and his family. Dear one reading this book — that is the grace we should be walking in today!

> *For the grace of God that brings salvation has appeared to all men, teaching us that, denying ungodliness and worldly lusts, we should live soberly, righteously, and godly in the present age, looking for the blessed hope and glorious appearing of our great God and Savior Jesus Christ, who gave Himself for us, that He might redeem us from every lawless deed and purify for Himself His own special people, zealous for good works.*
>
> — Titus 2:11–14

The life this Titus passage describes is like the life of Noah because we have the same life-saving grace of Abba Father to walk in today! We see the signs of population explosion, wickedness and evil, corruption and violence like never before on this planet! Just as redeemed Noah was zealous for the good work of building that lifeboat, we are to let grace teach us to build the life of Messiah in us — and everyone else we can possibly reach!

Hallelujah — like Noah, grace teaches us that the LORD will keep us from this time of great wrath. Remember, our Adonai Yeshua teaches there will be a time of trouble like nothing the world has ever seen. But like the bride in the Jewish wedding, we have the "Blessed Hope" — the hope of the glorious appearing of Savior Yeshua in the clouds, not only saving us from sin but also from the wrath and destruction of the tribulation period. Grace teaches us to look for this "Ark" of deliverance every day!

While many see the Rapture as a secondary matter, another great apostle sees it very differently. Peter, in his first letter, tells us to rest all our hope in the Rapture. Remember, the first time Messiah Yeshua will be revealed to us by sight will be in the clouds when He comes for us. What a great hope this is!

> *Therefore gird up the loins of your mind, be sober, and rest your hope fully upon the grace that is to be brought to you at the revelation of Jesus Christ...*
> — 1 Peter 1:13

A great way to end this chapter is to hear Paul teaching Yeshua's followers in one of his letters to the Thessalonians. The word was out that these special disciples had a powerful testimony of grace. They were looking for the "Blessed Hope"!

For they themselves declare concerning us what manner of entry we had to you, and how you turned to God from idols to serve the living and true God, and to wait for His Son from heaven, whom He raised from the dead, even Jesus who delivers us from the wrath to come.

— 1 Thessalonians 1:9–10

CHAPTER 10

Watch Therefore and Be Ready — The Faithful Servant

And what I say to you, I say to all: "Watch!"
                                        — Mark 13:37

We have seen Messiah Yeshua thoroughly answer His disciples in the first century regarding end-times scenarios. However, these warnings, as they pertain to those living now, are proving to be even more significant and essential to embrace. The best thing about this very sobering news (the signs He gave) is that our Adonai also gives us clear action items upon which to act with urgency. Bottom line: He tells us what to do to empower us for success, as we are the generation about which He spoke!

Watch therefore, for you do not know what hour your Lord is coming. But know this, that if the master of the house had known what hour the thief would come, he would have watched and not allowed his house to be broken into. Therefore you also be ready, for the Son of Man is coming at an hour you do not expect.
                                        — Matthew 24:42 – 44

What are we to do in light of Israel and the Nations' "Birth Pains," "the Fig Tree Generation," and "the Days of Noah"? First, we are to watch for the coming of Messiah Yeshua in the clouds for His people (the Rapture). Our watching should be accompanied by an urgency to be ready for His coming — like the bride who was prepared for the groom to return at any time.

One important recommendation is to not receive any teaching or doctrine that tries to convince you that Messiah Yeshua cannot come in the clouds for us today. Why is that? More is coming to clarify that issue, but for right now, remember that Messiah Yeshua warns that He is coming at an hour that people do not expect. With that in mind, when should we be ready for Him to come? Right now — always — every day! False doctrines teach that Adonai cannot come for us today — so why be ready today?

Some hold a "mid-trib or "post-trib Rapture" position. This means that Messiah Jesus cannot return in the clouds for His people until the middle or end of the "tribulation." The tribulation refers to the time Messiah spoke of as the season of the worst trouble ever on earth.

Let's consider a good answer that could bring harmony to a potentially divisive discussion. What if one of my middle or post-tribulation friends asks what I would do if, on the tenth or the hundredth day of the tribulation, born-again believers in Yeshua are still here? My reply would be: "That is simple — I would watch for the Groom to come today and be ready." Of course, I would be very surprised that we were still here, but by grace — nothing would stop me from being the faithful servant!

I would then ask a question: "Since Messiah Yeshua told us to watch for Him to come and be ready and that He is coming at a time when most think He will not, don't you think it would be best to watch for Him to come today and be ready?" My prayer is that this way of thinking would bring some measure of harmony.

Watching for Messiah to come today — with the clear understanding that He could — keeps us from great deception and trouble. For those who have paid much attention to the many recent battles America and other NATO troops have fought in Afghanistan and Iraq, there is an object lesson. One of the strategies employed is the fight for the hearts and minds of local villagers. They want to "win their hearts and minds" to help NATO forces gain ground in the war. The same kind of war has been taking place against humanity since the Garden of Eden. The battle for hearts and minds of precious souls has been raging relentlessly. Our Savior Yeshua wants to save us and keep our hearts and minds to deliver us from destruction.

Watching for Messiah Yeshua to come for us is a strategy of war our Savior is employing to guard our hearts and minds. Satan and his demons have the same strategy because he is a counterfeiter. He wants to win our hearts and minds over to the things of this world and its false doctrines so that we will not be looking for our Savior in the clouds. This is strategically intentional, and the reason will be addressed in the next chapter.

Watching for the Groom to come in the clouds for His bride, to take us to the place He has prepared, empowers us to keep this New Covenant command: "*Therefore you also be ready...*" Since He has commanded us to watch and be ready, wouldn't that be the thing to do every day? It certainly has blessed my life!

> *In My Father's house are many mansions; if it were not so, I would have told you. I go to prepare a place for you. And if I go and prepare a place for you, I will come again and receive you to Myself; that where I am, there you may be also."*
>
> — John 14:2–3

The Faithful Servant — Watching, Ready, Wise, Blessed

Our Savior Yeshua continues giving instructions to His people, especially those in the generation immersed in these unmistakable signs! He gives the example of two servants. It is so important to understand that in this parable, there are not three, four, or five servants — only two. I believe the Lord is telling us that each of us is one or the other. My prayer for myself, my family, and all those I can influence in any way is that we would be the first of the two.

> *Who then is a faithful and wise servant, whom his master made ruler over his household, to give them food in due season? Blessed is that servant whom his master, when he comes, will find so doing. Assuredly, I say to you that he will make him ruler over all his goods.*
>
> — Matthew 24:45–47

The first two words ("who then") refer directly back to the verses that pertain to watching and being ready. This example tells us how to watch and be ready for the coming of Messiah Yeshua for His people. The most effective way is to be the "faithful servant."

The faithful servant who is watching and ready for the Master to return is also wise. The Bible clearly tells us many ways to be wise according to Elohim. Proverbs is a book of wisdom that is chock full of the fear of Adonai Yeshua. Those who fear and love Him can ask for wisdom, and Abba Father gives it freely.

> *The fear of the Lord is the beginning of wisdom, And the knowledge of the Holy One is understanding.*
> — Proverbs 9:10

> *If any of you lacks wisdom, let him ask of God, who gives to all liberally and without reproach, and it will be given to him.*
> — James 1:5

The world is increasingly behaving without wisdom and mocking Adonai. In a world of foolishness, where crazed, God-hating lunatics rush headlong toward Elohim's judgment, we need to be wise like Messiah commanded:

> *Behold, I send you out as sheep in the midst of wolves. Therefore be wise as serpents and harmless as doves.*
> — Matthew 10:16

The faithful servant has been entrusted with the responsibility to tend to the Master's house until He returns. These affairs are this servant's to manage in place of the Master — what a huge responsibility! The primary task as temporary ruler over the Master's household is to give the others "food in due season."

But wait a moment — how does being ruler over the affairs of the house only boil down to one small matter: "food in due season"? This term means so much more than it may seem at first glance. In an effort to help us fully understand this saying, we should read all of Psalm 104. This may take some extra time, but it will be time well spent. Please see the context of this incredible chapter of the Bible and do not miss the command for the faithful servant:

> Bless the LORD, O my soul!
> O LORD my God, You are very great:
> You are clothed with honor and majesty,
> Who cover Yourself with light as with a garment,
> Who stretch out the heavens like a curtain.
> He lays the beams of His upper chambers in the waters, Who makes the clouds His chariot,
> Who walks on the wings of the wind, Who makes His angels spirits,
> His ministers a flame of fire.
> You who laid the foundations of the earth, So that it should not be moved forever,
> You covered it with the deep as with a garment; The waters stood above the mountains.
> At Your rebuke they fled;

At the voice of Your thunder they hastened away. They went up over the mountains;
They went down into the valleys,
To the place which You founded for them.
You have set a boundary that they may not pass over,
That they may not return to cover the earth.
He sends the springs into the valleys; They flow among the hills.
They give drink to every beast of the field; The wild donkeys quench their thirst.
By them the birds of the heavens have their home;
They sing among the branches.
He waters the hills from His upper chambers;
The earth is satisfied with the fruit of Your works. He causes the grass to grow for the cattle, And vegetation for the service of man,
That he may bring forth food from the earth, And wine that makes glad the heart of man, Oil to make his face shine,
And bread which strengthens man's heart. The trees of the LORD are full of sap,
The cedars of Lebanon which He planted, Where the birds make their nests;
The stork has her home in the fir trees. The high hills are for the wild goats;
The cliffs are a refuge for the rock badgers. He appointed the moon for seasons;
The sun knows it's going down. You make darkness, and it is night,

In which all the beasts of the forest creep about. The
young lions roar after their prey,
And seek their food from God.
When the sun rises, they gather together And lie down
in their dens.
Man goes out to his work
And to his labor until the evening.
O LORD, how manifold are Your works! In wisdom
You have made them all.
The earth is full of Your possessions — This great and
wide sea,
In which are innumerable teeming things, Living
things both small and great.
There the ships sail about; There is that Leviathan
Which You have made to play there. These all wait for
You,
That You may give them their food in due season.
What You give them they gather in;
You open Your hand, they are filled with good. You
hide Your face, they are troubled;
You take away their breath, they die and return to
their dust. You send forth Your Spirit, they are created;
And You renew the face of the earth.
May the glory of the LORD endure forever; May the
LORD rejoice in His works.
He looks on the earth, and it trembles; He touches the
hills, and they smoke.
I will sing to the LORD as long as I live;
I will sing praise to my God while I have my being.
May my meditation be sweet to Him;

I will be glad in the LORD.
May sinners be consumed from the earth, And the
wicked be no more.
Bless the LORD, O my soul!
Praise the LORD!

— Psalm 104:1–35

This chapter explains the awesomeness of the Lord and how He has made and keeps everything. He does so according to His goodness and kindness. Messiah can do anything (and He does) and be everything (and He is) to His creation! In the context of giving them food in due season (Psalm 104:27 and similarly Psalm 145:15), the Psalmist writes of the LORD providing crops to harvest so people can eat. This is an expression of the goodness of our Messiah Jesus! He opens His hand, and people are filled with His goodness!

When we apply this to the faithful servant, we see a comprehensive responsibility much broader than feeding people food. The faithful servant has been left by Messiah Yeshua to bring the righteousness, glory, and goodness of Creator Yeshua into this dark earth! Through Savior Yeshua, we can know Abba Father, as Ruach HaKodesh (Holy Spirit), is working to bring the lost to Abba. Our Heavenly Father is also changing us into the image of Messiah.

In the beginning was the Word, and the Word was
with God, and the Word was God. He was in the
beginning with God. All things were made through
Him, and without Him nothing was made that was
made. In Him was life, and the life was the light of

men. And the light shines in the darkness, and the
darkness did not comprehend it.

— John 1:1–5

In this manner, therefore, pray:
Our Father in heaven, Hallowed be Your name. Your
kingdom come.
Your will be done
On earth as it is in heaven.

— Matthew 6:9–10

In this context, "giving them food in due season" is the faithful servant bringing Abba Father, Messiah Yeshua, and the Holy Spirit (the Kingdom of Elohim) into this dark world! The faithful servant is demonstrating through his very heart, mind, and life, the love and mercy of the Father through Messiah Yeshua. This servant of righteousness is bringing the glory of Adonai from Psalm 104 to the doorstep of precious souls (lost and saved) who desperately need Him every day!

Understandably, for those born and raised in America and other affluent countries, comparing the glory of our great Redeemer Yeshua to food may seem strange. However, if we remember the context of Psalm 104 and other Bible passages, this comparison becomes much more clear. A look at the people who wrote the Scriptures, their way of life compared to ours, and how Messiah Yeshua reveals Himself makes the "food-glory" analogy come to life!

Those living in Israel during Bible times lived very differently than so many today. They did not have microwave ovens, fast food restaurants, or massive grocery stores with food from all over the world at their fingertips anytime — day or night. The Psalmist of chapter 104 understood something we often forget: Food does not magically appear at the Grocery Supercenter.

I took a two-day trip in Israel by automobile down into the Negev (Israel's southern desert region) close to the Egyptian border. It was so desolate — like nothing I had ever seen in person. I was very thankful to have a well-maintained vehicle, plenty of fuel, and a cell phone (even though I was not sure if there was cell coverage). While in that wilderness environment, I was extremely thankful to not be wandering like millions of others — not exactly sure where we were going or how long it would take to get there. But most of all I was thinking: where is the food and water?

We get a sobering reminder of our great need for Elohim to keep us alive as we consider the children of Israel's journey through the wilderness. It is the exact opposite of how we live today as they constantly looked to our Creator for food and water. Truth be known — so should we!

> *"Yet He had commanded the clouds above, And opened the doors of heaven, Had rained down manna on them to eat, And given them of the bread of heaven. Men ate angels' food; He sent them food to the full."*
> — Psalm 78:23–25

Remember, Messiah Jesus told us to pray this way:

> *"Give us this day our daily bread."*
> — Matthew 6:11

Food helps us understand the Lord's glory so much that He ties feeding Israel (His people) to His glory. Savior Yeshua is the one full of glory who came the first time to His people and will come again in all His glory! They were having difficulty understanding exactly who was standing in their presence. So Messiah explains it this way:

> *"I am the bread of life. Your fathers ate the manna in the wilderness, and are dead. This is the bread which comes down from heaven, that one may eat of it and not die.*
>
> — John 6:48–50

> *"This is the bread which came down from heaven — not as your fathers ate the manna, and are dead. He who eats this bread will live forever."*
>
> — John 6:58

> *"And the Word became flesh and dwelt among us, and we beheld His glory, the glory as of the only begotten of the Father, full of grace and truth."*
>
> — John 1:14

The Lord gives us another important instruction regarding the faithful servant giving food in due season. It also demonstrates keeping the greatest commandment of loving the true and living God with all our hearts (Mark 12:30). Peter was receiving instructions from our Resurrected Savior:

"He said to him the third time, "Simon, son of Jonah, do you love Me?" Peter was grieved because He said to him the third time, "Do you love Me?" And he said to Him, "Lord, You know all things; You know that I love You." Jesus said to him, "Feed My sheep."

— John 21:17

"Who then is a faithful and wise servant, whom his master made ruler over his household, to give them food in due season? Blessed is that servant whom his master, when he comes, will find so doing. Assuredly, I say to you that he will make him ruler over all his goods."

— Matthew 24:45–47

The Blessed Faithful Servant

The faithful servant is also blessed! Why is he so blessed? It is because his watching, readiness, faithfulness, and wisdom have facilitated obedience to the Master. Think of it this way: the faithful servant is watching for the Master to return and doing what the Master commanded. When the Master returns, He will be pleased with the servant He left in charge. The reason the Master will be pleased is because when He returns, the servant will be doing exactly what the Master commanded.

What will be the obvious expression that the faithful servant is blessed? The Master will make him ruler over all His goods — what a blessing! The first appointment was a test that, once passed, blesses the faithful servant with an eternal position over the Master's house — Wow! And Hallelujah!

We have not yet observed the second servant in this parable. First, there are other analogies to see. They also convey the concept of servants and a traveling master, though with some distinctions. One distinction is that there are two faithful servants — not one. This conveys the idea that within the category of "faithful servant," there are different abilities. Some have greater capabilities while others have lesser, but faithfulness is the measure of success — quality not quantity.

> *For the kingdom of heaven is like a man traveling to a far country, who called his own servants and delivered his goods to them. And to one he gave five talents, to another two, and to another one, to each according to his own ability; and immediately he went on a journey. Then he who had received the five talents went and traded with them, and made another five talents. And likewise he who had received two gained two more also.*
>
> — Matthew 25:14–17

First, remember that we are hearing about how to live as a citizen of the kingdom of heaven — so often minimized today. The point is that our King and Master Yeshua has left us with an extremely high-priced investment. Individually, and corporately in the body of Messiah, we are to reach lost souls with the greatest treasure ever — the gospel of and discipleship in Messiah Yeshua!

We can see the value of the responsibility in human and temporal terms by the costly "goods" the servants were left to invest. A talent of gold in Israel at that time weighed about two hundred pounds or ninety-one kilograms. A talent of silver was about one hundred pounds or forty-five kilos. Whatever kind of commodity or currency this was — it was valuable.

And again, the master gave an amount according to the ability of each servant's capacity to invest it. Both of these servants behaved wisely with the master's goods and actually doubled the initial investment. As certain as the sun coming up in the morning, their master returned — what was his response to the servants' behavior?

> *So he who had received five talents came and brought five other talents, saying, 'Lord, you delivered to me five talents; look, I have gained five more talents besides them.' His lord said to him, 'Well done, good and faithful servant; you were faithful over a few things, I will make you ruler over many things. Enter into the joy of your lord.' He also who had received two talents came and said, 'Lord, you delivered to me two talents; look, I have gained two more talents besides them.' His lord said to him, 'Well done, good and faithful servant; you have been faithful over a few things, I will make you ruler over many things. Enter into the joy of your lord.*
>
> — Matthew 25:20–23

The master says their jobs have been well done, and he calls them good and faithful servants! These servants of righteousness (heaven's standard of goodness) have passed the test of the "few things" and now will receive promotion into the "many things." Actually, the faithful servants are told they will be "rulers over many things." Also, they are welcomed to enter the joy of their lord. The implications of these faithful servants' rewards are so exciting and abundantly relevant!

Dear one reading — right now, we are to be investing the Master's goods! Our Adonai Yeshua left on a journey to prepare a place for us. Until He returns, our Lord and Savior has commanded us to be watching, ready, faithful, wise, obedient, and blessed Kingdom investors. Now, just before Master Yeshua returns, we have the final opportunity to be faithful in the few (temporal as opposed to eternal) things of this life.

Faithful servants of Messiah Yeshua will be rulers over many things in the Kingdom of Adonai. In Luke 19, the Lord gives a similar parable regarding a ruler and his servants. The "many things" rewarded are identified as cities. The faithful servants become rulers over cities based on their faithfulness to the nobleman, or master.

> *Then came the first, saying, 'Master, your mina has earned ten minas.' And he said to him, 'Well done, good servant; because you were faithful in a very little, have authority over ten cities.' And the second came, saying, 'Master, your mina has earned five minas.' Likewise he said to him, 'You also be over five cities.'*
>
> — Luke 19:16–19

When our Master, King Messiah Yeshua, returns, we will return with Him to rule and reign under His Lordship. We will be regional rulers based on the degree to which we have been like these faithful servants. Our faithful service now will determine what we will rule over then. Very specifically, Messiah tells the first Jewish apostles exactly where they will be reigning:

> *And I bestow upon you a kingdom, just as My Father bestowed one upon Me, that you may eat and drink at My table in My kingdom, and sit on thrones judging the twelve tribes of Israel.*
> — Luke 22:29–30

The Joy of the Lord and the Suffering Servant

Along with the blessing of ruling over many things, the invitation to enter the joy of his Lord is also extended to the faithful servant. What does this mean, "to enter into the Joy of your Lord"? It is so very powerful!

It is impossible to imagine what it was like for our Suffering Savior to leave heaven and come to this wretchedly dark place. Consider how He became the most righteous man ever to live in such an evil world. Then, think of the abuse to which He submitted Himself, as He loved those He came to save, enough to allow them to accuse, curse, mock, beat, and crucify the King of Glory like a criminal, or actually more like an animal.

Yet, the separation from Abba Father on the cross was the worst horror this eternal Adonai experienced, or ever would. So then, here is a question: what was the primary thing that sustained Messiah Yeshua during this time of immeasurable sorrow? The answer is written in a passage that was given to help us (His disciples) through times of trouble:

> *Therefore we also, since we are surrounded by so great a cloud of witnesses, let us lay aside every weight, and the sin which so easily ensnares us, and let us run with endurance the race that is set before us, looking unto Jesus, the author and finisher of our faith, who for the joy that was set before Him endured the cross, despising the shame, and has sat down at the right hand of the throne of God.*
>
> — Hebrews 12:1–2

The Prophet Isaiah's writings contain what are called "the Four Servant Songs." They are writings about the Holy Suffering Servant who would come to save Israel and the nations from their sins. This One who would come to suffer would have to be faithful beyond measure. Afterward, He would be exalted to the highest position in heaven.

> *Behold, My Servant shall deal prudently;*
> *He shall be exalted and extolled and be very high. Just as many were astonished at you,*
> *So His visage was marred more than any man,*
> *And His form more than the sons of men..."*
>
> — Isaiah 52:13–14

In this passage, we see Messiah Yeshua was beaten so severely that His appearance was changed significantly (His visage was marred). He would have been gruesome to behold.

Then we see Him exalted. Our Lord is similarly prophesied in Isaiah 53 over seven hundred years before His appearance as a man on earth.

> *Surely He has borne our griefs And carried our sorrows;*
>
> *Yet we esteemed Him stricken, Smitten by God, and afflicted.*
>
> *But He was wounded for our transgressions, He was bruised for our iniquities;*
>
> *The chastisement for our peace was upon Him, And by His stripes we are healed.*
>
> *All we like sheep have gone astray;*
>
> *We have turned, every one, to his own way;*
>
> *And the LORD has laid on Him the iniquity of us all. He shall see the labor of His soul, and be satisfied.*
>
> *By His knowledge My righteous Servant shall justify many, For He shall bear their iniquities.*
>
> *Therefore I will divide Him a portion with the great, And He shall divide the spoil with the strong, Because He poured out His soul unto death,*
>
> *And He was numbered with the transgressors, And He bore the sin of many,*
>
> *And made intercession for the transgressors.*
>
> — Isaiah 53:4–6, 11–12

Our Savior had a sustaining influence that helped Him endure the cross and shame. Our Suffering Servant Messiah was strengthened because He would "see the labor of His soul, and be satisfied," as Isaiah says. This is the joy that was set before Him, spoken of in the previously mentioned Hebrews passage.

To better understand "the joy that was set before Him," we need to answer a question. What was the mission on which Messiah was sent? It was to be Abba Father's Faithful Suffering Servant!

> *For God so loved the world that He gave His only begotten Son, that whoever believes in Him should not perish but have everlasting life.*
>
> — John 3:16

> *...for the Son of Man has come to seek and to save that which was lost.*
>
> — Luke 19:10

> *Therefore, holy brethren, partakers of the heavenly calling, consider the Apostle and High Priest of our confession, Christ Jesus, who was faithful to Him who appointed Him, as Moses also was faithful in all His house.*
>
> — Hebrews 3:1–2

Abba Father sent Messiah Jesus to seek and save the lost of this world. He faithfully paid for humanity's sins on the cross. Our great Savior Jesus was faithful to Abba Father and accomplished the mission of redemption. Our Adonai Yeshua then stepped into the joy set before Him. He was established as the Good and Faithful Servant of Abba Father.

The Faithful Servant
Suffers with His Master

Remember the word that I said to you, 'A servant is not greater than his master.' If they persecuted Me, they will also persecute you. If they kept My word, they will keep yours also.

— John 15:20

Another expression of being the faithful servant is that he is so closely identified with His Master that he incurs the same kind of suffering. The early apostles, and then Paul, understood this and actually welcomed a closer association with Messiah's suffering. As far as the world is concerned, it is guilt by association — what an honor!

And they agreed with him, and when they had called for the apostles and beaten them, they commanded that they should not speak in the name of Jesus, and let them go. So they departed from the presence of the council, rejoicing that they were counted worthy to suffer shame for His name. And daily in the temple, and in every house, they did not cease teaching and preaching Jesus as the Christ.

— Acts 5:40–42

That I may know Him and the power of His resurrection, and the fellowship of His sufferings, being conformed to His death...

— Philippians 3:10

In like manner, Messiah is calling for faithful servants all over the world. He was sinless and perfectly followed Abba Father's plans. This qualifies anyone who has the Spirit of Messiah in them to be good and faithful servants. His warnings clearly show us that like at no other time, we should be the watching, ready, faithful, wise, and blessed servant. We can operate according to the gifts and opportunities given to us by our Master, who might return at any time.

Afterward, we can enter into the joy of our Lord, having accomplished the mission for which our Master has called us. Having taken the path of our Suffering Servant Master as good and faithful servants, we will experience His promotion. Through eternity, we will then be established to reign and rule under King Messiah Yeshua! The alternative is the second servant of the Matthew 24 parable and the third servant of the Matthew 25 parable.

CHAPTER 11

The Wicked Servant

But if that evil servant says in his heart, 'My master
is delaying his coming...'
— Matthew 24:48

When I was a little boy, I remember my precious Jewish mother sitting at my bedside and discussing the coming of Messiah. I asked her something like this: "If all these signs of the Lord's coming will be shaking the earth, how will people not see that Yeshua is coming?" She answered something like this: "Because the world will be so dark and will love their sin so much they will not be able to see that He is returning." Her words were so profound, and as we see today, also tragically include most of those who profess faith in Messiah Yeshua.

We have looked at the "faithful servant" and his characteristics. The "wicked servant" of the same parable also has very clearly defined ways about him. Sometimes, we need to be taught and reminded what not to do.

But if that evil servant says in his heart, 'My master
is delaying his coming,' and begins to beat his fellow
servants, and to eat and drink with the drunkards,
the master of that servant will come on a day when

*he is not looking for him and at an hour that he is not
aware of, and will cut him in two and appoint him
his portion with the hypocrites. There shall be weeping
and gnashing of teeth.*

— Matthew 24:48–51

The Wicked Servant Isn't Watching

The "wicked servant" is such a terrible option to choose, especially compared to the "faithful servant." He truly is the opposite in every way, so there can be no legitimate confusion regarding the two. First, the wicked servant is not watching today for the Lord to return in the Rapture.

Before going any further, it is important to note that I am NOT asserting in any way that all who believe the mid or post-tribulation Rapture doctrine are the wicked servant. All three camps (pre, mid, and post-trib) have people who are both the faithful and wicked servants. Some pre-trib folks believe that Messiah will come in the clouds before the tribulation period, but still are the wicked servant because, in their hearts, they are not looking for Him because they are not the faithful servant. Theirs is simply an intellectual ascent that is not motivated by faith.

Additionally, I have met mid and post-trib believers who are the faithful servant. For example, there are geographic regions and church cultures where believers in Messiah Jesus have never heard sound teaching on the pre-trib position. It is something they have never considered as they have grown up spiritually in a dogmatic mid or post-trib environment. They have shared with me the longing in their heart for the coming of the Lord and expressed hope in a pre-trib Rapture. These precious ones live for Messiah Jesus every day looking forward to His return, yet, because of their end times doctrinal upbringing, they do not believe that He could come today.

The wicked servant believes the Master is delaying His coming because he doesn't want Him to return. This unrighteous servant loves this present world and the things that are in it. He worships himself and the creation, not the Creator. The Bible clearly speaks about the heart of this servant:

> *Do not love the world or the things in the world. If anyone loves the world, the love of the Father is not in him. For all that is in the world — the lust of the flesh, the lust of the eyes, and the pride of life — is not of the Father but is of the world.*
>
> *— 1 John 2:15–16*

> *…who exchanged the truth of God for the lie, and worshiped and served the creature rather than the Creator, who is blessed forever. Amen.*
>
> *— Romans 1:25*

The Wicked Servant Against the Faithful Servant

"…and begins to beat his fellow servants…"
— Matthew 24:49

Adonai Yeshua tells us this servant begins to beat His fellow servants. If you look down through history, beginning with Cain and Abel, you will see the wicked servant persecuting the faithful servant. So it is today. While the faithful servant is watching for the Master to return and doing what the Master commanded, what effect does that have on the wicked servant?

He feels condemned because he is, and that conviction often provokes a response. Noah condemned the world by preparing for the flood, so the wicked servant feels condemned by the Rapture!

> *By faith Noah, being divinely warned of things not yet seen, moved with godly fear, prepared an ark for the saving of his household, by which he condemned the world and became heir of the righteousness which is according to faith.*
>
> — Hebrews 11:7

Entire books have been written on the subject of the religious, including professing Christians, who have horribly persecuted the faithful servant. This is an ancient reality that is still with us today. Sadly, within the body of Messiah, there is a tangible trend of heightened aggressiveness against watching for Messiah to come now, before the tribulation.

Here is one almost unbelievable example. I have friends who were invited to a Messianic Erev Shabbat (Friday evening Sabbath) dinner. A discussion began regarding the Rapture, and when my friends identified themselves as pre-trib, they were asked to leave. The hosts considered that doctrinal position to be such heresy that their brother and sister in Messiah were no longer welcome. Why were they in such trouble? It is because those who were asked to leave are faithful servants watching for the Master to come today — because He might!

The Wicked Servant Is Worldly

"...and to eat and drink with the drunkards..."
— Matthew 24:49

Not only is the wicked servant not watching for the Rapture and persecuting the faithful servant, he also would rather associate with the godless — even drunkards. The old saying aptly applies: "Birds of a feather flock together." He has little thought or concern for the returning Master because he would rather have fellowship with those who walk in darkness.

The Unfruitful Wicked Servant Cannot Invest the King's Resources

But he who had received one went and dug in the ground, and hid his lord's money.
— Matthew 25:19

As we consider the other servant parable from Matthew 25, we see that the wicked servant has no interest in investing the Master's resources. It would stand to reason that the wicked servant is also unfruitful. In this parable, the wicked servant could care less about the returning Master. This demonstrates that, though having been called, he is not chosen.

You did not choose Me, but I chose you and appointed
you that you should go and bear fruit, and that your
fruit should remain, that whatever you ask the Father
in My name He may give you.

— John 15:16

Messiah Yeshua calls His people with a very specific purpose — to be fruitful. He chooses and appoints all His followers to bear eternal fruit. This produce represents the souls that are saved, disciples that are made, other believers who are built up and encouraged, and Yeshua's light that shines in the darkness through our lives! The wicked servant has no interest in bearing fruit, which is an expression of his identity — the "Wicked Servant."

The Wicked Servant and the Master's Return

After a long time the lord of those servants came and
settled accounts with them.

— Matthew 25:19

It is inevitable — the Master is returning! Though many try to disbelieve it away, come He will. "After so much time, certainly, it must just be a myth" or "Never mind these signs all around us — Messiah Yeshua may not come back for another 2,000 years" are the ways so many think. For many, maybe even most, in church today, a tragic surprise awaits them.

Having lived lives hoping the Master will not return, He will do so at a time many think that He will not. And when

He comes, this parable teaches that all accounts will be settled. The many years of living as the wicked servant will be over. A new and eternal existence is now here.

The Wicked Servant Goes to Hell and the Lake of Fire

For decades, during and after the 60s and 70s, the so-called "Jesus Movement" in America, the Rapture of believers was a hot topic. There was a book and movie series in the 90s called *Left Behind*, whose authors and their teams went around speaking in churches. One Sunday night, I was at a packed church of about 1,500 people who'd come to hear a speaker from the team.

This precious man of God came to the pulpit trembling as he began to ask forgiveness from all in attendance. He asked that we forgive him on behalf of so many pastors who had not told the truth about hell. I will never forget his brokenness and humility as he unpacked the horrors that await so many.

Though most congregations do not have meetings on Sunday evenings anymore, when they did, most everyone who attended was already a born-again believer in Messiah Jesus. Yet after hearing the truth about hell for forty minutes, many who were only "make believers" held up their hands and prayed to receive Yeshua as Adonai!

For the "itching ears" generation in which we live, hell is most often left out of the teaching. It certainly does not fill the pews with financial givers and happy "members in good standing" (MIGS). But have "Christians" been complicit in filling hell? This may be a good question to consider. For that is exactly where the wicked servant is going, whether he or she be one of the MIGS or not. Hell is described in the Bible as a destiny after this life with very specific characteristics. Though not pleasant to look at, it would be foolish to ignore.

> *The master of that servant will come on a day when he is not looking for him and at an hour that he is not aware of, and will cut him in two and appoint him his portion with the hypocrites. There shall be weeping and gnashing of teeth.*
>
> — Matthew 24:50–51

Not much displeases the Lord more than religious hypocrisy. This dressing up in pretend religious exercise is harmful to so many. Not only do such actors not have authentic faith, but hypocrites also keep others from saving faith in Messiah Yeshua. They are complicit in Satan's work of sending people to hell. This is why they must also go there.

> *But woe to you, scribes and Pharisees, hypocrites! For you shut up the kingdom of heaven against men; for you neither go in yourselves, nor do you allow those who are entering to go in. Woe to you, scribes and Pharisees, hypocrites! For you travel land and sea to win one proselyte, and when he is won, you make him twice as much a son of hell as yourselves.*
>
> — Matthew 23:13–15

> *Serpents, brood of vipers! How can you escape the condemnation of hell?*
>
> — Matthew 23:33

The hypocritical wicked servant goes to a place called hell. The word "hell" comes from the name of an actual place in Israel from New Testament Bible times. "Gehenna" was in the valley of Hinnom, south of Jerusalem, where they burned trash and the bodies of dead animals. This is a fitting name to describe this horrible destiny of the pretending servant.

In Gehenna, there will be weeping and gnashing of teeth for two primary reasons. One is the torment and suffering. The wicked servant would not be identified with the suffering of Messiah in the temporal life, so he will experience the suffering and torment of rejecting the only hope of forgiveness of sin — the love of the Master Messiah Yeshua.

The wicked servant is given an eternal body that will endure the flames of hell. Like the burning bush in the Torah book of Exodus, which was on fire but not consumed, so it will be with the wicked servant. Messiah gives an account of a time when a rich man, who lived luxuriously in this life, trades places with a beggar in the next life. The beggar is in Abraham's bosom — a temporary paradise until after the resurrection of Messiah, who brought those in Abraham's bosom to heaven. The rich man is in hell.

> *And in hell he lift up his eyes, being in torments, and seeth Abraham afar off, and Lazarus in his bosom. And he cried and said, Father Abraham, have mercy on me, and send Lazarus, that he may dip the tip of his finger in water, and cool my tongue; for I am tormented in this flame.*
> — Luke 16:23–24 (KJV)

The other reason is the utter despair of knowing that kind of torment is their final destiny. The final sentencing, after the one-thousand-year reign of Messiah, will be the Great White Throne Judgment. This is where all those in hell will be sentenced and transferred to the eternal Lake of Fire.

> *Then I saw a great white throne and Him who sat on it, from whose face the earth and the heaven fled away. And there was found no place for them. And I saw the dead, small and great, standing before God, and books were opened. And another book was opened, which is the Book of Life. And the dead were judged according to their works, by the things which were written in the books. The sea gave up the dead who were in it, and Death and Hades delivered up the dead who were in them. And they were judged, each one according to his works. Then Death and Hades were cast into the lake of fire. This is the second death. And anyone not found written in the Book of Life was cast into the lake of fire.*
> — Revelation 20:11–15

So many today are laughing their way into hell — even celebrating it. But when they realize that they cannot leave — ever — their laughter will turn to weeping. Truly, this will be the end of the line, the most hopeless existence possible. There is no way out of the eternal sentence that begins in hell!

CHAPTER 12

Judgment Seat of Messiah: Eternal Rewards and Loss

For we must all appear before the judgment seat of Christ...

— 2 Corinthians 5:10

Having spent a significant amount of time in many different circles of the body of Messiah in many countries, I can say something with a measure of experience and authority: there is too little teaching on the judgment seat of Messiah, which is evident in the thinking and living of too many disciples of Adonai Yeshua. If we would only begin to understand the gravity of this event, it would make big changes in our lives!

For we must all appear before the judgment seat of Christ, that each one may receive the things done in the body, according to what he has done, whether good or bad. Knowing, therefore, the terror of the Lord, we persuade men; but we are well known to God, and I also trust are well known in your consciences.

— 2 Corinthians 5:10–11

Think of it, if you are a disciple of Messiah Jesus, you will appear before Him to be judged. For clarification, this judgment is not to determine innocence or guilt. Everyone at this judgment has been declared righteous and eternally forgiven for their sin.

Each of us will stand individually before the Lord to be scrutinized for our deeds done in this temporary life in these temporary bodies. The things we have done that are good will be distinguished from those that are bad. Paul also warns about the terror of the Lord, which is a good reminder — the fear of the Lord is the beginning of wisdom.

We rarely hear about this, but for those born again who stubbornly refused to grow in grace, this will be a horrifying event. If you have a problem with that, just refer back to the verse just quoted: *"Knowing, therefore, the terror of the Lord, we persuade men..."* We need to remember that during this life, the Ruach HaKodesh (Holy Spirit) reminds us so many times and in so many ways to repent and pursue the things of the Kingdom of God. It will be a startling moment when these people learn that they will enter into eternity having lost out on their rewards and eternal positions.

You see, we live in a modern society that believes in false gods, even false Jesus Christs, that are corrupt like we naturally are corrupt. But when we stand before the true and living King Messiah Jesus, as the old saying goes, "All will come out in the wash."

However, a more accurate observation tells us that instead of things coming out in the wash, they will be tested by fire. All that we have done as believers in Messiah will be tested by fire to determine something that will be very personal and irrevocably eternal. Paul speaks about this matter to the same church in his first letter. He uses the analogy of a builder. You and I are builders of one thing or another. Our work will be tested to determine the quality.

Rewards and Losses

For we are God's fellow workers; you are God's field,
you are God's building. According to the grace of God
which was given to me, as a wise master builder I
have laid the foundation, and another builds on it.
But let each one take heed how he builds on it. For no
other foundation can anyone lay than that which is
laid, which is Jesus Christ.
— 1 Corinthians 3:9–11

Paul speaks of the Corinthian Church as Elohim's field and building. The apostle to the Gentiles has labored in that harvest and built according to God's grace given to him. All believers in Adonai are to work in the field and build upon that foundation of Messiah Yeshua. No other legitimate foundation can be laid because Yeshua is the way, the truth, and the life and the only cornerstone!

Now if anyone builds on this foundation with gold,
silver, precious stones, wood, hay, straw, each one's
work will become clear; for the Day will declare it,
because it will be revealed by fire; and the fire will test
each one's work, of what sort it is.
— 1 Corinthians 3:12–13

All true believers in Adonai Yeshua start off building upon the foundation of salvation He has provided for us. Then, by grace, we are to cooperate with His working in our lives. We are expected to do so by authentic personal discipleship including, but not limited to, reading and living His word, prayer, and fellowship in the body of Messiah.

After the Rapture, as we stand before Messiah at this judgment, our labor as His disciples will be tested by fire (for the Day will declare it "because it will be revealed by fire") On that Day, it will become very clear how we have spent our lives in Messiah! And what is the purpose of all this?

> *If anyone's work which he has built on it endures, he will receive a reward. If anyone's work is burned, he will suffer loss; but he himself will be saved, yet so as through fire.*
>
> — 1 Corinthians 3:14–15

The Holy Spirit's breathed word tells us that our authentic work will endure the testing and will also be rewarded. The things done badly will burn up and will result in loss of rewards. We also learn in other passages that the rewards are very tangible and understandable. This is important in that today, we can know what to look forward to on "that Day."

There are insightful passages in which we find faithful servant crowns that are awarded to those who have passed through the judgment seat of Messiah. These crowns are not temporary and are rewards for very specific concepts and categories, so there should be no confusion for those who really want them. Sadly, so many believers today care more for a perishable crown.

> *And everyone who competes for the prize is temperate*
> *in all things. Now they do it to obtain a perishable*
> *crown, but we for an imperishable crown.*
> — 1 Corinthians 9:25

> *And also if anyone competes in athletics, he is not*
> *crowned unless he competes according to the rules.*
> — 2 Timothy 2:5

The upward call of Abba Father in Messiah Jesus should be considered the primary goal for everyone who claims the name of our Lord Jesus! This goal comes with a prize, like that won by an athlete who has prepared to compete with excellence according to the rules. Of course, one aspect of this prize pertains to the reward of a crown or crowns.

> *Not that I have already attained, or am already*
> *perfected; but I press on, that I may lay hold of that for*
> *which Christ Jesus has also laid hold of me. Brethren,*
> *I do not count myself to have apprehended; but one*
> *thing I do, forgetting those things which are behind*
> *and reaching forward to those things which are ahead,*
> *I press toward the goal for the prize of the upward call*
> *of God in Christ Jesus.*
> — Philippians 3:12–14

The upward call of our Heavenly Father in Messiah Yeshua focuses on sowing His Word in the lives of His people. Messiah came to save and bless precious souls. If we truly love our Lord and Savior Yeshua, we will also love people. Paul loved and lived for the benefit of others.

> *Therefore, my beloved and longed-for brethren, my joy and crown, so stand fast in the Lord, beloved.*
> — Philippians 4:1

> *For what is our hope, or joy, or crown of rejoicing? Is it not even you in the presence of our Lord Jesus Christ at His coming?*
> — 1 Thessalonians 2:19

Just think of it: because our Lord and King wore a crown of thorns, we have the opportunity to receive eternal rewards and wear crowns in His kingdom! Below are examples of some of those available to us. We should live the life of Messiah in us today so that we may receive crowns in the future.

The Crown of Righteousness

> *Finally, there is laid up for me the crown of righteousness, which the Lord, the righteous Judge, will give to me on that Day, and not to me only but also to all who have loved His appearing.*
> — 2 Timothy 4:8

It is fitting that the crown of righteousness is given by the righteous Judge — the Lord Messiah Yeshua. It will be given on that Day to all those who have loved the appearing of Messiah Yeshua in the clouds as He fetches His bride. Tragically, there will be some at the judgment seat who have His righteousness but did not truly abide in Him in this life. They will actually be ashamed when He comes because they did not walk out their faith when given the opportunity. It will be too late once the righteous Judge appears in the Rapture.

> *And now, little children, abide in Him, that when He appears, we may have confidence and not be ashamed before Him at His coming.*
> — 1 John 2:28

Let's continue to consider why the crown of righteousness is given to those who love His appearing. All who come to this judgment have His righteousness — right? Those who love His appearing, like the faithful servants who invested wisely, will be excited to present the increased investments to their returning Master; therefore, they were anticipating His return with overflowing excitement.

Those who are living righteously and godly in this present age are doing the same. They almost cannot wait to present full baskets to the One who called us to bear fruit that will remain! This makes me want to get to work in His field of harvest.

Those who fruitfully abide in Him will be full of unspeakable joy when the Lord appears! They will have a good day at the judgment seat of Messiah. They (I pray — we) will receive the crown of righteousness as we love His appearing!

The Crown of Life

*Blessed is the man who endures temptation; for when
he has been approved, he will receive the crown of life
which the Lord has promised to those who love Him.*
— James 1:12

*Do not fear any of those things which you are about to
suffer. Indeed, the devil is about to throw some of you
into prison, that you may be tested, and you will have
tribulation ten days. Be faithful until death, and I
will give you the crown of life.*
— Revelation 2:10

Satan is the father of lies. He has so many different schemes
devised to separate us from our powerful witness and then our
rewards. Thankfully, our Father in heaven uses these evil at-
tempts against us to prove our genuine faith and generously
reward us!

Whether by temptation or persecution, our Heavenly Father empowers us to pass the tests. Even if this means being
faithful to death, it will be worth it all when we receive the
crown of life! There are a couple of go-to passages that help me
in times of testing:

*My brethren, count it all joy when you fall into vari-
ous trials, knowing that the testing of your faith pro-
duces patience. But let patience have its perfect work,
that you may be perfect and complete, lacking nothing.*
— James 1:2–4

No temptation has overtaken you except such as is common to man; but God is faithful, who will not allow you to be tempted beyond what you are able, but with the temptation will also make the way of escape, that you may be able to bear it.

— 1 Corinthians 10:13

The Crown of Rejoicing

For what is our hope, or joy, or crown of rejoicing? Is it not even you in the presence of our Lord Jesus Christ at His coming?

— 1 Thessalonians 2:19

As mentioned earlier, making faithful servant disciples of Messiah Jesus through evangelism, soul winning, and ongoing discipleship is a win/win eternal investment! It secures crowns for others and ensures great rewards for one's self. Having prioritized the discipleship of others in this life, think of the joy and sense of personal satisfaction as we see them receive their rewards from the Lord. In this context, to then be crowned by our King and Savior for doing so will certainly make this a "crown of rejoicing!"

The Crown of Glory

Shepherd the flock of God which is among you, serving as overseers, not by compulsion but willingly,

*not for dishonest gain but eagerly; nor as being lords
over those entrusted to you, but being examples to the
flock; and when the Chief Shepherd appears, you will
receive the crown of glory that does not fade away.*
— 1 Peter 5:2–4

Now more than ever, believers in Messiah Yeshua need faithful leaders who really love the Lord enough to want to feed His sheep. In these "Days of Noah," it seems so many professing shepherds are more interested in poisoning and fleecing His sheep. However, there is good news.

In every generation, including this one, the Great Shepherd has faithful shepherds who truly love and feed the flock. Faithful shepherds need support and encouragement in these corrupt and wicked days. Our King has a great reward for which authentic church leaders can anticipate with joy.

Keep Your Crown!

As we have already seen, the judgment seat of Messiah primarily involves reward and loss. Also, we just looked at the thief and how he plans to steal our rewards. However, our Savior has provided a way for us to overcome and not lose our rewards. Our Father in Heaven gives good gifts and will make the way for His children to win!

*Now thanks be to God who always leads us in tri-
umph in Christ, and through us diffuses the fragrance
of His knowledge in every place.*
— 2 Corinthians 2:14

Behold, I am coming quickly! Hold fast what you have, that no one may take your crown. He who overcomes, I will make him a pillar in the temple of My God, and he shall go out no more. I will write on him the name of My God and the name of the city of My God, the New Jerusalem, which comes down out of heaven from My God. And I will write on him My new name.

— Revelation 3:11–12

Wow, believers in Adonai Yeshua are always on the winning path as we walk in the way of righteousness. We are also admonished to hold fast to what we have so that nobody steals or takes our crown! Those who overcome will receive the incredible rewards listed in this passage. We know that Satan came to steal, kill, and destroy. We must overcome this threat, but specifically, how do we do so?

And they overcame him by the blood of the Lamb and by the word of their testimony, and they did not love their lives to the death.

— Revelation 12:11

The way we walk out our God-given victory is by our faith in Messiah Yeshua, who shed His precious blood and rose from the grave! We walk out our faith abiding in our King Jesus, who gives us a life that is powerfully full of His grace and mercy. This overcoming life gives witness that Yeshua is alive. We walk out our faith in Messiah, choosing even death if necessary — and for some, it is. This is how we overcome and keep our crown!

Crowns and Eternal Positions

Around the throne were twenty-four thrones, and on the thrones I saw twenty-four elders sitting, clothed in white robes; and they had crowns of gold on their heads.

— Revelation 4:4

The twenty-four elders fall down before Him who sits on the throne and worship Him who lives forever and ever, and cast their crowns before the throne, saying:
"You are worthy, O Lord,
To receive glory and honor and power; For You created all things,
And by Your will they exist and were created."
— Revelation 4:10–11

These elders represent those "in Messiah Yeshua" who have been caught up. By way of reminder, Paul said that those in Messiah would be caught up after having heard a trumpet blast and the heavenly shout. Not only do they have crowns, they sit on thrones. Remember, those who endure and suffer with Messiah Yeshua also reign with Him (2 Timothy 2:12).

The One who created all things has rewarded His people with crowns and thrones. We see them on earth before the Rapture in the first chapter of Revelation. We then see them in heaven in the above Revelation 4 passage and in the fifth chapter of Revelation:

John, to the seven churches which are in Asia:

Grace to you and peace from Him who is and who was and who is to come, and from the seven Spirits who are before His throne, and from Jesus Christ, the faithful witness, the firstborn from the dead, and the ruler over the kings of the earth.

To Him who loved us and washed us from our sins in His own blood, and has made us kings and priests to His God and Father, to Him be glory and dominion forever and ever. Amen.

— Revelation 1:4–6

Now when He had taken the scroll, the four living creatures and the twenty-four elders fell down before the Lamb, each having a harp, and golden bowls full of incense, which are the prayers of the saints. And they sang a new song, saying:

"You are worthy to take the scroll, And to open its seals;

For You were slain,

And have redeemed us to God by Your blood Out of every tribe and tongue and people and nation, And have made us kings and priests to our God; And we shall reign on the earth."

— Revelation 5:8–10

Their (our) ruling and priestly assignments have been given, having passed through the judgment seat of Messiah. True believers in Messiah Yeshua will return to take up their positions in His kingdom! Oh, what we have to look forward to — amen!

Some may wonder why these are eternal positions and think that somehow they can later regain what was lost at the judgment seat. There is a very simple reason why this cannot be the case. It should provoke us all to walk by faith.

Once we see our Savior and enter into His reign on earth, there is something that we will never do again: we will never again live by faith. The requirement for eternal rewards that are given to Messiah followers is based on how we walk out our faith in Him. Always keep this passage on your dashboard:

> *But without faith it is impossible to please Him, for he who comes to God must believe that He is, and that He is a rewarder of those who diligently seek Him.*
> — Hebrews 11:6

The Omnipotent Groom and the Spotless Bride

And I heard, as it were, the voice of a great multitude, as the sound of many waters and as the sound of mighty thunderings, saying, "Alleluia! For the Lord God Omnipotent reigns! Let us be glad and rejoice and give Him glory, for the marriage of the Lamb has come, and His wife has made herself ready." And

to her it was granted to be arrayed in fine linen, clean
and bright, for the fine linen is the righteous acts of the
saints.

— Revelation 19:6–8

After all the centuries of creation's suffering in the futility of
sin, the heavenly hosts rejoice as that which was hoped for is
finally realized. Not only does Adonai Elohim Omnipotent
reign in heaven, His prophetic plans for heaven coming to
earth with His bride are about to come to pass! What is the
word of this rejoicing — Alleluia!

This celebration, in large part, is for the marriage quite literally made in heaven. The Groom has come for His bride, she
has been made ready at the judgment seat of Messiah, and all
that remains of her is pure righteousness! All the righteousness
that she hungered and thirsted for in the earthly life is finally
fulfilled reality in the eternal life! All that remains of those who
mourned for their sins is righteousness and sinlessness. Truly,
the most important prayer has been practically and eternally
answered — "Lord Yeshua, please deliver me from my sins!"

Then he said to me, "Write: 'Blessed are those who are
called to the marriage supper of the Lamb!'" And he
said to me, "These are the true sayings of God."

— Revelation 19:9

For all who seek after temporal things and esteem them
highly as blessings from heaven, this should be a wake-up call.
This beckoning is to come up higher — Hallelujah! The call is

to the marriage supper of the Lamb. This is the true blessing to be sought for in this life.

The Warrior Groom, His Warrior Bride, and Israel Born Again!

The nations of the world, having followed Antichrist during this time, are under the fierce wrath of the Warrior Lamb, Yeshua. The nations are closing in on Jerusalem to destroy Israel and kill the Jews. Yet the Lamb is about to personally introduce Himself in another way to the wicked God-hating world that has come against Him for so long. He is now going to fulfill His covenants in grand fashion. The Warrior Groom — and at His side, His Warrior Bride — is dressed for battle, and He is coming with His blood of the New Covenant!

> *Now I saw heaven opened, and behold, a white horse. And He who sat on him was called Faithful and True, and in righteousness He judges and makes war. His eyes were like a flame of fire, and on His head were many crowns. He had a name written that no one knew except Himself. He was clothed with a robe dipped in blood, and His name is called The Word of God. And the armies in heaven, clothed in fine linen, white and clean, followed Him on white horses. Now out of His mouth goes a sharp sword, that with it He should strike the nations. And He Himself will rule them with a rod of iron. He Himself treads the winepress of the fierceness and wrath of Almighty God.*

And He has on His robe and on His thigh a name
written: King of Kings and Lord of Lords.

— Revelation 19:11–16

At last, the King has come to sit on the throne of David! His Bride, who is not unaccustomed to warfare, has come to witness this great victory and take up her position with the reigning King! The first order of business is to strike Israel's enemies with the sharp sword of His word. The second — save Israel from their sin! It is at this time that all of Israel who have survived the great tribulation are saved — according to covenant.

For I do not desire, brethren, that you should be ig-
norant of this mystery, lest you should be wise in your
own opinion, that blindness in part has happened to
Israel until the fullness of the Gentiles has come in.
And so all Israel will be saved, as it is written:
  "The Deliverer will come out of Zion,
   And He will turn away ungodliness from Jacob;
For this is My covenant with them,
   When I take away their sins."

— Romans 11:25–27

And I will pour on the house of David and on the
inhabitants of Jerusalem the Spirit of grace and
supplication; then they will look on Me whom they
pierced. Yes, they will mourn for Him as one mourns

for his only son, and grieve for Him as one grieves for
a firstborn.

— Zechariah 12:10

The Faithful Groom and the Rewarded Bride!

The book of Revelation begins with the Groom speaking to His betrothed on earth — the churches before the Rapture. And what does the Groom say toward the end of John's prophecy, not only to those in the book of Revelation but to all Bible-believing churches?

> *And behold, I am coming quickly, and My reward is*
> *with Me, to give to every one according to his work. I*
> *am the Alpha and the Omega, the Beginning and the*
> *End, the First and the Last.*
> — Revelation 22:12–13

As we have seen, just as promised, we can know right now to some degree the kind of rewards that are available to us. We can get to work right now in the Kingdom of Elohim, knowing these crowns and positions await us. We have also been warned of great loss for not being Messiah's co-laborers. He who has always been, is now, and will always be, has given us His word!

Truly, the word from Isaiah 64:4 given to the Corinthians is for us today. The great desire of our covenant-keeping Heavenly Abba Father is to reward us on "that Day." As we close this final chapter together, here is another verse of Scripture that describes what the Holy Spirit is revealing to those who love Him:

> *But as it is written:*
> *"Eye has not seen, nor ear heard,*
> *Nor have entered into the heart of man*
> *The things which God has prepared for those who love*
> *Him." But God has revealed them to us through His*
> *Spirit. For the Spirit searches all things, yes, the deep*
> *things of God.*
> — 1 Corinthians 2:9–10

With this in mind, what should we remember? Each day is a new opportunity to prepare for the Master to return. The faithful servant is looking every day for Him to do so. While he is watching, this wise and blessed servant is also doing what the Master commanded. He has taken the Master's command very seriously: WATCH THEREFORE AND BE READY!

A Born Again Faithful Servant Lifestyle

- Daily Loving Messiah Yeshua and Looking for the Rapture (Luke 10:27, Titus 2:13)
- Daily Loving People-Start at Home (Luke 10:27)
- Daily Praising Messiah Jesus (Psalm 147:1)
- Daily Prayer (1 Thessalonians 5:17)
- Daily Bible Reading (Psalm 119:105)
- Frequent and Regular Church Attendance/ Fellowship Relationships (Hebrews 10:25)
- Frequent Use of Spiritual Gifts in the Body of Messiah (1 Corinthians 12, Romans 12, 1 Peter 4, Ephesians 4)
- Frequent Fasting and Prayer (Matthew 6:17–18 "…*when you fast…*")
- Frequent Gospel Sharing (We are ALL Gospel Ambassadors, 2 Corinthians 5:17–21)
- Frequent Discipleship-Start at Home (Matthew 28:18–20)
- Frequent Financial Giving to the Kingdom's Work (Luke 6:38)

About the Author

Dov Schwarz is an American/Israeli Jewish believer in Messiah Jesus.

He is the founder of Watch Therefore Ministries, and under this umbrella organization, he also co-founded the ministry Blessing Israeli Believers.

Dov has founded another Kingdom work — *Poured Out for the Nations* — through which he has ministered multiple times in ten different African countries. There, he preaches the gospel, makes disciples, works with church planters, and ministers to orphans and widows.

Dov Schwarz has been an associate pastor of a denominational church and a church-planting pastor of Calvary Chapel Beth Shalom — now Calvary Chapel Pearland. Both are in the Houston, TX, area. He has also authored four other books: *America's Ark: The Only Safe Place for Americans Today*, *The Gospel Truth About the Rapture*, *Activate the Blessings of the Abraham Covenant*, and *Identity Crisis Israel and The Church*

Dov Schwarz Contact Information:

- EMAIL: dovforisrael@gmail.com
- WEB: www.watchtherefore.tv

Endnotes

1   J. Dwight Pentecost, *Prophecy for Today: The Middle East Crisis and the Future of the World* (Grand Rapids: Zondervan, 1961), 20–21.

2   White, Matthew, "Necrometrics: Estimated Totals for the Entire 20th Century," Historical Atlas of the Twentieth Century, 2010, http://necrometrics.com/all20c.htm.

3   Christian Persecution And Genocide Is Worse Now Than "Any Time In History," Report Says, http://www.newsweek.com/christian-persecution -genocide-worse-ever-770462.

4   Russell, David, "Statistics," SURF Survivors Fund, https://survivors-fund.org.uk/awareness-raising/statistics/.

5   Barnard, Anne, "Death Toll from War in Syria Now 470,000, Group Finds," *New York Times*, February 11, 2016.

6   "Zero Hunger," World Food Program, http://www1.wfp.org/zero-hunger.

7   "Oklahoma Becomes Earthquake Capital of the World," Yahoo! News, https://www.yahoo.com/news/video/oklahoma-becomes-earthquake-capi-tal-world-042754045.html.

8   Oskin, Becky, "Big Earthquakes Double in 2014, but They're Not Linked," Live Science, June 27, 2014, http://www.livescience.com/46576–more -earthquakes-still-random-process.html.

9   Quakes Are Increasing, But Scientists Aren't Sure What It Means, https://www.latimes.com/local/ la-me-la-quakes-20140603-story.html

10   Worldwide Surge in "Great" Earthquakes Seen in Last 10 Years (10) https://www.nbcnews.com/science/ science-news/worldwide-surge-great-earthquakes- seen-past-10-years-n233661

11   https://www.usgs.gov/faqs/why-are-we- having-so-many-earthquakes-has-naturally- occurring-earthquake-activity-been

12   http://www.numberofabortions.com

13   Obama Uses Sermon On The Mount To Elevate Speeches https://www.christianitytoday.com/ct/2009/ aprilweb-only/116-51.0.html